KEYS TO PARENTING AN ADOPTED CHILD

Kathy Lancaster, M.A.

BARRON'S

Cover photo by Scott Barrow, Inc., Cold Spring, NY

All inquiries should be addressed to:
Barron's Educational Series, Inc.
250 Wireless Boulevard
Hauppauge, New York 11788

Library of Congress Catalog Card No.: 95-20864

International Standard Book No. 0-8120-9104-3

Library of Congress Cataloging-in-Publication Data
Lancaster, Kathy.
     Keys to parenting an adopted child / by Kathy Lancaster.
       p.   cm. — (Barron's parenting keys)
     Includes bibliographical references and index.
     ISBN 0-8120-9104-3 (pbk.)
      1. Children, Adopted. 2. Parenting. I. Title. II. Series.
HV875.L22   1996
362.7'34—dc20   95-20864
                                     CIP

PRINTED IN THE UNITED STATES OF AMERICA
6789   9770   987654321

CONTENTS

INTRODUCTION: THE PARENT-CHILD RELATIONSHIP

The parent-child relationship is very personal. Our children—whether they come to us through birth or adoption—are like no other children in the world. They are influenced by our habits and interests, our strengths and weaknesses, even our subconscious mannerisms. At the same time, they develop their own unique characteristics, which we are powerless to change.

Some adults see parenting as a relatively simple equation of love and discipline. Others believe that successful parenting is a more complex process that deals with a multitude of issues that unfold during a child's growth and development. Regardless of the complexity of the formula, the goal is happy, well-adjusted children who become happy, well-adjusted adults.

Even after the adoption of our own children, we may have thought that adoption added only subtle differences to the parenting process. We may have believed that most adoption issues were significant only for children who are visibly adopted, that is, whose physical features mark them as genetically unrelated, or for children with special needs related to the circumstances surrounding their reasons for adoptive placement. If our children joined our family through a same-race infant adoption, we may have presumed that adoption issues could be handled comfortably within the home and that our greatest challenge would be in deciding when and how to tell them that they were adopted. Good parenting skills, we believed, would handle the rest.

The public and private denial of differences by adoptive parents is certainly not uncommon. It was, in fact, the societal stance about adoption during the greater part of this century. Many adopters continue to believe that a "keep the door closed" policy will shield their children from hurt and protect the family from the stigma of adoption. Their fears, they admit, are not based on concern that the children may be reclaimed by birthparents, or worry about the loss of the children's love or the threat of divided loyalty, or even the children's possible confusion over adoption issues. What many adoptive parents fear is the loss of the perception of the family unit "as it should be."

Our desire to put aside parent profiles, passports, photolists of adoptable children, and other reminders of the adoption process (see *Keys to Adopting a Child* by Kathy Lancaster, Barron's, 1994) and get on with the business of being a family is understandable. Yet the experiences of both adult adopted persons and mental health professionals tell us that greater attention to adoption issues is in order. All adopted children struggle at one time or another with issues related to their adoptive placement. They may express their conflicts to their parents or they may keep them internal, but all adopted children deal with such questions as "Why didn't my first parents want me?" and "Who am I, really?"

These questions are normal and natural, and they serve to help our children achieve balance with their role as adopted persons in society. As parents, we must help our children understand the reasons behind their adoptive placement, emphasize their role in the family, and validate the true difficulty of their birthparents' situation before placement.

For the sake of our children we should not deny—even implicitly by not bringing up the issue—that our children have a different genetic heritage from our own. Our communication about adoption to our children must be an ongoing process that is open yet unobtrusive. Our goal must be to help our children achieve harmony among their genetic history, self-identity, ethnic heritage, and adoptive family bonds.

Many people believe that success in raising our children is a measure of a life well spent. Indeed, this may be our greatest legacy. As my father said to me, "You've done a lot of good things in your life. But the very best was raising this little boy."

Part One

▼▼▼

ADOPTION SUCCESSES

L ike all children, our adopted children come to us as developing beings. To help them grow into healthy, well-adjusted adults, we need to understand the issues that they face and provide them with unconditional love and encouragement.

We all want to succeed in parenting our children. More importantly, we want our children to succeed. One way to analyze the process of raising well-adjusted children is by examining the young people and adults who have successfully adapted to life as adopted persons. By looking at their successes, we can uncover many of the separate components that contributed to their well-being.

Analyzing Adoption Success

In the largest study of adoptive families in the United States to date, researchers for the Search Institute compared Midwestern teenagers who were adopted as infants to their non-adopted brothers and sisters. This analysis, published in *Growing Up Adopted* (Benson et al., 1994), examined the health and well-being of all of the teenagers involved in the study. They found that the majority of the adopted children are as happy and well-adjusted as their non-adopted brothers and sisters. Like the majority of all adolescents, the children who were adopted either domestically or internationally are mentally healthy.

The study shows that the factors that contribute to the success of these adopted adolescents are strong attachments, solid families, and positive communication about adoption issues.

Time and again, these are the success factors, whether the children are of the same or a different race than their adoptive parents, whether they were adopted as infants or older children, and whether or not other adoption risk factors are present.

To achieve that success for our own children, we need to dedicate our energies to developing these factors. What is important for children is permanence and stability, unconditional love, and the recognition of the importance of their experiences and prior relationships.

Perhaps the best measure of both our success and our children's success is to compare what their lives would have been like if they had not been adopted. Adoption, even if it occurs after infancy, is almost always better than the alternative.

1

ADOPTION—WHAT TO EXPECT

A doption adds a level of complexity to the life of an adopted person. The loss that results from displacement, even at an early age, hurts children. Adoption risk factors, such as a history of abuse or multiple moves, add to the wound.

Whatever the issues are that affect your child, you can be assured that they will surface at varying times in his development. How he deals with these issues and, in fact, makes adoption just an accepted fact of his life will largely depend upon his feelings of belongingness in your family.

If we are to help our children successfully adjust, we need to understand and then help our children accept three fundamental precepts:

1. Every adopted child was born to a woman, and that woman grieved when the child left her.
2. The actions or decisions of birthparents (or other adults in any prior placements) were not the fault of the child.
3. Each adopted person has a different genetic and social history (and possibly a different cultural heritage or an existence of past relationships) than other adoptive family members yet is an important and valued member of the family.

Normal Crises

Normal, predictable crises happen in the development of all family relationships. Whether the crisis is perceived as positive or negative—a job change, the birth of a child, a move to a new neighborhood—certain predictable changes will occur within the formation and growth of a family.

For adoptive families, even in the least complicated situations, crises are equally normal and predictable. The ups and downs of psychological adaptation can be anticipated for even the most well-adjusted adopted persons. Certain issues can be expected to surface at certain stages of development. It is important to understand these issues, even to predict them, so they can be placed in a context that allows them to be seen as normal.

Issues related to adoption are complicated, but they are not necessarily problems. The best solution is a preventive approach and the realization that not all crises are negative. Then when crises surface that do require professional intervention, parents are better prepared to seek professional assistance for their children without overreacting to the behaviors, assessing blame, or assuming guilt.

Negative Images

What is behind the popular notion that adopted persons never really fit in? that they are more likely to seek professional help for emotional difficulties? that they are apt to encounter problems in forming healthy relationships and seem to have a greater likelihood of social maladjustment?

Certainly there may be negative influences on the mental health of some adopted persons. They include:

- a lack of attachment to significant people in their lives,
- the influence of dysfunctional families, and
- the effects of poor communication about adoption.

4

Although it may be true that adopted persons are more likely to seek professional counseling, there are a number of possible explanations.

First, adoptive parents may be more likely to seek counseling services for their children because of the family's exposure to mental health professionals during the adoption process. Parents may feel comfortable about these professionals and their services. They may also believe that the success of their own adoption process was influenced by pre- and post-placement counseling services. They may want to continue that link to success by using mental health services as they feel the need arise. The family may also believe that the use of mental health services, including support groups, is an asset rather than a stigma.

Second, adoptive parents may feel unsure about their parenting skills. They may be more likely to call a therapist about their three year old's fear of bedtime monsters, for example, than a non-adoptive parent who decides that a lot of three year olds are afraid of monsters or that Uncle Joe was that way, too. Adoptive parents may feel especially vulnerable when their children express an interest in meeting their birthparents or finding out more about their very early life experiences.

A third possible explanation of a greater incidence of emotional difficulties for adopted children is the hurt that brings some children to adoptive placement in the first place. In fact, the studies that point toward a higher rate of referral may not separate clients adopted as infants from those who were adopted at a later age; thus, adoption may not be the only difference.

Regardless of the number of adopted children who use mental health services or the reasons behind the referrals, the majority of those children who do receive such services are very healthy. In other words, the families who ask for help are the ones who succeed in helping children.

Successful Adjustment

In its study of children adopted as infants and their non-adopted brothers and sisters, the Search Institute identified a number of characteristics of well-adjusted teens. Whether adopted or non-adopted, these teens perform well in school, they have educational goals for the future, they feel a connectedness to their parents and friends, they care about others, they feel good about themselves socially, and they expect to be happy and successful adults.

Obviously these are admirable qualities worthy of any child's effort and any parent's pride. When children feel comfortable with their adoptive status and secure with their role in the family, they are as likely to be well-adjusted, happy, contributing members of society as children who are raised by their biological parents.

2

WHAT IT IS LIKE TO BE ADOPTED

C hildren carry in their souls the early knowledge of not being chosen by their birthparents. Throughout their lives they reach for connections—for people who look like them, for the people who gave them life.

Adopted children and adults deal with divided loyalties and confusion. They have questions about their conception and the reasons for adoptive placement. They face confusion about their identity and their role in the family and in society. At one time or another they experience all of the strong feelings of grieving, including sadness, despair, guilt, shame, anger, rage, and resolution.

As the institution of adoption changes, so will the experience of being adopted. As you might expect, feelings about adoption differ from person to person and from age to age. Some people will focus on continued questioning and self-doubt—"Why did this happen to me?" Others key on the positive aspects—"This is something that happened to me beyond my control. I can be happy that I have been given another chance." The common issues of isolation, a search for self, and a sense of a lost past and lost relationships occur so frequently, though, that they can be described as ongoing challenges for all adopted people.

What are the most effective coping aids? Time, preparedness, and acceptance. Time to heal. Preparedness for the predictable stages of feeling that commonly result from such an experience. Acceptance that adoption is a fact of their life.

Normal Patterns of Adjustment

A wide range of emotions can be described as normal reactions to adoption that still lead to a healthy, well-adjusted life. As varied styles of adoption become more common, it will be harder to make generalizations about what it is like to be adopted.

There is no right or wrong way to adjust to the fact of being adopted; however, this individuality of adjustment also contributes to feelings of isolation.

The search for self is an important aspect of the adoption experience. It is, in fact, an important aspect of any person's growth and development. The struggle to figure out who you are, where you fit in, and what you will become is universal. For adopted people, a major difference in their search for self is that a part of them has been cut away.

The sense of a lost past and lost relationships is complicated for adopted people. Adoption loss is more extensive, less socially recognized, and more penetrating than other losses that children experience, such as the death or divorce of their parents.

For many adopted people, grieving for past relationships is an emotion that is frequently misread by adoptive parents. The emotions and behaviors that children display in reaction to these losses are often misinterpreted as laziness, learning disabilities, or even lack of intelligence rather than as grief over the loss of a past and past relationships.

The amount that any one adopted person will grieve adoption issues is unpredictable. Sometimes grieving becomes a significant factor in an adopted person's life. Sometimes it

8

does not. Both reactions, though, are natural and understandable parts of a healthy adjustment to adoption.

Grieving adoption issues is an emotion that adopted people may experience at different stages during their lifetime. In fact, the amount that any one person focuses on adoption issues will change over the course of her life. Sometimes the issues will be a primary concern. At other times, the subject of adoption will be comfortably tucked away while the individual focuses on other important issues.

Another normal reaction is an interest in meeting birthparents. Adopted individuals express two main reasons for seeking information about and meeting their birthparents, especially their birthmothers:

1. *Need for knowledge.* They want to find out what their birthparents were like—their interests, talents, and, most important, their physical features. The comment that searching adults frequently express is a desire "to find someone who looks like me" and to find a physical measure of what they might become.
2. *Affirmation.* Adopted people also express a yearning to tell their birthparents that they are okay, that the decision for adoption resulted in a good life for them.

Some adopted people carry their interest in meeting their birthparents forward and conduct a search. Others do not. A successful search can have many definitions and may or may not result in direct contact with birthparents. For some adopted people, the act of searching may be cathartic. The search may, in fact, be the true search for self rather than for lost biological relatives. Even if relatively little information is available about the birthparents, adopted people can benefit from visiting or learning more about their birthplace and cultural origins.

9

Lifetime Feelings

Feelings about adoption change from the time an adopted person is first able to think about her unique family status until old age, when she makes a final effort to blend her feelings about adoption into an integrated sense of self. The experience of adoption is not static. It changes with time as individuals grow and develop. The issue of being adopted is one that an adopted person will return to, both consciously and unconsciously, many times during her lifetime.

3

ADOPTIVE FAMILIES

M any adults, adoptive parents included, believe that parenting is parenting whether families are built by birth or adoption. They believe that effective parents accept their children as they are, look for the children's own unique qualities, and provide love, security, and guidance. To a great degree, this is true.

Adoptive families are different than families built through birth, however. Parents of a biological child who steals must decide how to deal with and prevent repeated incidents. Parents of an adopted child who steals may wonder about "bad blood" and take him to a child psychologist. As much as we try to avoid it, the question surfaces again and again: Is this normal or is this adoption?

A large number of studies have shown that bonding between mother and infant is the same whether the child was born to the mother or adopted. Although adoptive parents will attest that the loving attachment is the same in adoption, practically everything else is not the same.

Differences

To help our children successfully adapt, we must acknowledge the differences between adoptive and biological families and take positive steps to incorporate adoption education into our family system.

Differences in Adoptive Families

1. Most adoptive parents have dealt with the stresses of infertility and evaluations by adoption professionals about their ability to be good parents.
2. Many have spent large sums of money and a great deal of time in order to adopt.
3. Unlike biological parents, who have greater control of influences on their children—choosing a mate and prenatal care, for example—adoptive parents have little input into their children before they enter the family.
4. Adoptive parents must grapple with deciding when and how to disclose the fact of their children's adoption.
5. They worry about their children's acceptance by family and society.
6. They must deal with their children's questions about identity and genetic history and, in some cases, the influences and the memory of past relationships.

It is important to note that all of these issues are ongoing. Infertility issues do not end with adoption. They surface when the parents tell their children about their adoptive status. They surface again when the adopted children conceive and give birth. Likewise, issues of acceptance continue. A grandchild adopted transracially may be accepted equally as a biological grandchild—until he reaches puberty and wants to date and marry someone of his own race. The cycle of all of these issues will be to emerge and fade and emerge and fade throughout a lifetime. For adoptive parents, the overall effects of the differences will tend to fade. For adopted children, they will tend to grow.

Assumptions

Some adoptive parents operate under a set of assumptions about adoption issues and their importance in the lives of their children.

One of these assumptions is that the love of adoptive parents can meet all of a child's needs. "No one could love this child more than I," we explain. While that statement is valid, it is incorrect to extend that to mean that parental love can meet all of our children's needs. As much as we love our children, our love cannot compensate for their losses through adoption.

A second assumption pertains to the character of birthparents. Many adults, even many adoptive parents, believe that birthparents really do not care about the welfare of their children. This view about uncaring birthparents is as common in infant placements as it is in older-child adoptions.

Whether adoptive placement is voluntary or involuntary, all birthparents have a level of concern and caring for their children. They may not make their feelings known to anyone. They may deny those feelings to themselves. In some cases, the birthparents may even have behaved in ways that were severely detrimental to the children. However misguided (or criminal) those behaviors may have been, it bears repeating that on one level or another all birthparents love and care about the children they conceive and bear, and they grieve the loss of those children.

The Critical Issue for Children

It is critical that our children know and understand that their birthparents loved them and felt sad when they left. Even if a child is the product of rape, incest, or attempted abortion, in order for that child to feel a sense of self-worth, he must be made to feel that his birthparents had a measure of innate value and that they grieved his loss. (If you cannot believe this measure of birthparental love, accept it for the sake of your child and his need for a link to humanity.)

An attitude that suggests that all adoptive parents are loving and that birthparents were uncaring does not benefit our children. It denies that they have other needs, needs that adoptive parents cannot meet no matter how hard they try, and it also denies children the humanness of their birth identity.

The true issue for our children is not the amount of parental love we provide. Nor is it the character of their birthparents. For the sake of our children, the single most important issue must be helping them establish a connectedness to humanity.

Early identity concepts are formed through feelings connected to genetic family, the circumstances of birth, and early life experiences. As adoptive parents, if we deny, ignore, or degrade these influences, we undermine our children's good feelings about themselves. We must provide the linkage—past to present to future—that makes our children feel secure.

Helping Children

Whatever the reactions of parents may be, adopted children *are* different from birth children. Helping children means that parents must first accept these differences.

It may be beneficial for parents to reexamine their reasons for choosing adoption and, if necessary, readdress unresolved infertility issues. This allows parents to accept both a lack of genetic connection and the fact that their children have different genetic histories. It also enables parents to let go of a fantasy-child mold into which they may be trying to force their children.

Parents also need to recognize the impact of the children's experiences of separation from their birth families and the permanent change in destiny that adoption brings. Recognition of differences may also include facing extended family members who may not accept the children, especially if the children are of a different race or ethnic heritage.

We can help our children understand these adoption issues and come to terms with them and their feelings about them. This involves helping the children find appropriate ways to express their feelings about adoption and learn how to deal with distressing matters related to adoption.

Successful adoptive parenting also means examining our own expectations of the parent-child relationship. Sometimes that which we most expect from our children may be what is most difficult for them to give. A parent's desire for love, affection, and family harmony may be great on certain holidays—Mother's Day, for instance. These may be the very times when the children are least able to express those feelings.

Your child may be struggling with his own memories (or absence of memories) and questions of loyalty and belonging. A simple acknowledgment of his feelings on these holidays can be beneficial. Words of acceptance, such as "I'll bet Mother's Day reminds you of the time that you spent with your mother Anne. Do you think about her often?" honor the role of the missing person and validate the child's feelings about the prior relationship.

Death and Divorce

The death or divorce of parents is difficult for any child. For adopted children who have already faced loss, abandonment, and disruption, the death or divorce of their parents adds feelings of extra loss, extra abandonment, and extra disruption. Children react in different ways to this "second" loss of a caregiver, depending on their age, developmental stage, and history of prior trauma.

Guilt is an especially strong emotion for adoptive parents who divorce. They worry about the additional disruption in their children's lives. Commonly their guilt is intensified with concern that they have violated the faith that agencies or birthparents placed in them and that their children will somehow feel responsible for the adults' failed relationship.

Regardless of the circumstances, parents must deal with their own grief and new challenges while trying to comfort and provide stability to their children. Parents can help their children understand and accept the situation by explaining the situation in nonjudgmental terms that the children can understand.

Parents who divorce need to work hard to separate with a minimum of strife and to show their children that it was the adult relationship that did not work, not the children's relationship with either parent. Those relationships can continue to be maintained through shared custody and visitations. Above all else, children need to understand that despite the changed structure of the family, their place in the family is secure.

Strengths of Adoptive Families

Adoptive families have a great many strengths. Most adoptive parents were required to examine their motives for parenting before placement. Determined to become parents and to provide healthy, nurturing families for their children, they tend to enjoy parenting and to work hard at it. Without a genetic connection to their children, they tend to accept each child for who he is rather than to bring preconceived expectations to the parent-child relationship. In general, they are strong, stable, and accepting individuals who have made a commitment to their children. They believe that adoption is a wonderful, enriching experience. Above all, they make significant positive impacts on the lives of their children.

4

NATURE AND NURTURE

Some adopted children grow up to resemble their birth-parents. Others take after their adoptive parents. The vast majority of children show the influences of both their birth and adoptive families.

Most modern researchers believe that personality is a result of biology *and* experiences, that children inherit a range of characteristics that is strongly influenced by their environment. Simply put, people are born and then they are shaped.

The real question is no longer whether human personality is influenced by genes or environment, but how the two relate. Studies have shown that heredity accounts for approximately 50 percent of a person's personality (25 percent is inherited from each parent), and nongenetic factors account for the other 50 percent (30 percent is due to environmental factors and 20 percent is due to parenting style).

Genes influence certain traits—how vulnerable children are to stress, how motivated they are to achieve, their leadership skills, their career interests, and their hobbies, for example. Environment influences how children use those traits—how they deal with conflict and how they develop their skills and talents.

Children's personalities are determined by the mixing of their genetic programming and their day-to-day environment. Inherited traits can be positively influenced by an environment that stimulates children or negatively influenced by a deprived environment. Physical strength, an inherited trait, might equip your daughter to be successful athletically. But whether she turns out to be a street fighter or a downhill skier is more influenced by her environment than her genetic programming.

The task for parents is to accept their children's genetic programming and channel it toward its greatest potential.

Hereditary Traits

Physical features are strongly influenced by genetics. Hair color, eye color, skin color, body build, physical strength, skill development, and coordination and balance are determined genetically. Genetics also influences certain kinds of diseases, impairments, and problems in development. The potential for addiction and delinquent behavior is genetically influenced to a lesser degree.

Intelligence, learning styles, disposition, and aptitudes are also genetically influenced—your child's artistic talent, for example, or her interest in classical music.

Personality Traits—Strong Genetic Links

extroversion	conformity
anxiety	creativity
paranoia	cautiousness
aggressiveness	optimism
ambitiousness	orderliness
friendliness	shyness
curiosity	charm
flexibility	

Personality Traits—Weaker Genetic Links
self-esteem
relationship patterns
capacity for intimacy

Accommodating Differences

One way of using scientific evidence about the genetic influences on children is to look at family building in a new light. Whether children enter families through birth or adoption, it is not the children's task to accommodate the vision of the parents in order to build ideal families. It is the task of parents to provide permanent, nurturing families for children.

Many adoption advocates believe that modern family building should be built on the plan that, first, we discover who the children are. Next we figure out how to accommodate who they are. Finally we figure out how we can work together to help them be the best they can possibly be.

As parents, we can provide experiences that positively shape our children's genetic tendencies. Children who inherit physical strength or thrill-seeking behaviors have an opportunity to direct those characteristics into socially useful behaviors—to become firefighters rather than felons, for example. With such genetic programming, however, we cannot expect to shape these little people toward championship chess. The task is not to stamp out the traits but to recognize them and to channel them into socially acceptable activities.

Genetic tendencies toward health problems can be influenced by modifications in diet and exercise. Psychological disorders can be improved by attention to constructive changes, such as positive experiences, interventions, low stress, and positive self-esteem. Unfortunately, however, we cannot completely change the genetic programming of any individual child.

Using Genetic Information

Parenting children who are genetically unrelated may present challenges. Adoptive parents face raising children who may have many fundamental differences, including

19

personalities and temperaments that are at odds with the dispositions of the parents and other family members.

All genetic information about adopted children is incomplete. The usefulness of any genetic information lies in determining how the information will help us support, nurture, and parent these particular children.

5

~~~~~~

PRIVACY AND NORMALCY

A doptive parents are excited about adopting. We are excited about our children and excited about adoption. Despite our understandable enthusiasm, it is important that we consider our children's privacy and that we set some boundaries about what we will reveal to others.

Children have the right to privacy regarding their status as adopted persons in society and the details of their history before placement. They also have the right to grow and develop as normal children without undue emphasis on the fact of their adoptive status.

As difficult as it may be to contain our enthusiasm about adoption, it is more important that information about children's birth families and their pre-adoption histories not be shared with anyone outside the family unless the information is needed by professionals who are caring for the children. Parents who indiscriminately provide such information breach the children's right of privacy. Regardless of whether the information is considered positive or negative, it may come back to adversely affect the children.

Your Child's Rights

Your child's adoptive status need not and should not define him legally, publicly, or socially. He has the legal rights of a biological child in your family. Siblings in the family are his legal brothers and sisters. He has an equal place on the family tree and in inheritance matters. Beyond that, the circumstances of his adoption are personal matters.

One good rule of thumb in dealing with the personal details of your child's life is not to discuss with anyone outside the immediate family details that you have not shared with your child. This holds true in infant adoptions as well as older child adoptions. Think twice about revealing any information about your child, or a prospective child, that may be considered negative. This is private information. When your child is old enough to understand details related to his adoptive placement, he has the right to decide what information he wishes to share.

Remember that neither you nor your child is compelled for any reason to answer questions about the adoption, any more than you are compelled to answer questions about any other personal matters (your finances, for instance). You and your child have the right not only to make decisions about how you want to answer questions but about whether you want to answer them at all.

Your Responsibility
Children need to feel that they belong, that they are accepted, and that they are attached. That connectedness is reinforced by the answers that parents give to questions about their children's adoption. It is important to realize that you owe no friend or stranger an answer. What you owe is affirmation of your child as a member of your family.

Your job is to parent your child. You do not have to be an ambassador for adoption by providing information to the curious. Your responsibility is to help your child grow and develop into a healthy, well-adjusted adult.

Unfortunately we cannot shield our children from the losses of adoption, the stigma of adoption, or prejudice against minorities in our society. What we can, and must, do is empower our children by teaching them to handle life's inequities and to deal with the difficulties they encounter. This involves helping children establish self-identity, self-esteem, and mechanisms for handling conflicts.

We are also responsible for making our children feel a connectedness to our families. We do this through *claiming*, or identifying ways our children are like us, and *entitlement*, or developing a sense of belongingness in our children. For children who were adopted at an older age and who have faced too many changes, this means that we must focus on building relationships with them.

The Need for Boundaries

The general public is extremely curious about adoption and tends to take greater liberties with the privacy of adopted children than with non-adopted children. The general public also tends to take greater liberties with children who are racially different from their adoptive families. These liberties take the form of either probing questions or invasion of the children's personal space. Inappropriate actions are frequently veiled under the guise of curiosity or misguided appreciation of the benevolence of adoptive parents.

People who ask inappropriate questions or invade your child's personal space are disrespectful and should be corrected. You will need to learn to identify these inappropriate behaviors and how to intervene on your child's behalf.

Society in general expects negative behaviors from adopted people. Any information about your child's background that may be considered negative is likely to fuel fires of negative expectations. A child whose birthparents were felons may prompt gossip about the genetics of criminality, for example.

Inappropriate Comments

Families whose children are visibly adopted are more likely to encounter public stares and questions than families with adopted children who are racially similar; however, no family is immune to inappropriate questions about adoption.

Unfortunately, inappropriate stares and questions are frequently aired in the presence of the children. Questions such as "Where did she come from?" or "Are they really brother and sister?" are not uncommon. (For ideas on helping children answer questions about adoption, see Key 14.)

These questions may or may not be ill-intended. They may be poorly phrased attempts by prospective adopters who are interested in building a family like yours. Your best approach is to discuss with your child how he would like to answer the questions. If possible, prepare for these questions in advance.

Families do not need to shield their adopted children from insensitive remarks as much as they need to reaffirm the children's place in the family through their responses to such remarks.

Physical and Emotional Boundaries

Physical and emotional boundaries tend to be weaker for children who are visibly different from their parents. Minority children in a white family are frequently subject to inappropriate invasion of personal space. People tend to be more familiar with minority children, touching their heads or caressing their hair, for example, than they would with children who are the same race as their families. These actions occur more frequently and for a more prolonged period for minority children in a family than for racially similar children.

Such attitudes suggest that this behavior is acceptable since society has already set the children aside as being unusual and, therefore, not subject to the same rules of conduct as other children.

Privacy also includes emotional boundaries to which all individuals are entitled. Introducing the children as "our adopted sons" is as inappropriate as introducing birth children by their method of entry into the family, such as "our Caesarean-section sons." Singling out children because of their adoptive status—by blaming adoption or birth relatives for negative behaviors, for example—unfairly labels the children and burdens them with responsibility for events that are beyond their control.

At School

Opinions vary on the advisability of revealing children's adoptive status to school officials. On one hand, access to the information may help school personnel better deal with adoption-related issues that may arise. On the other hand, there may be fear of some sort of prejudicial treatment based on the children's adoptive status.

Whichever path you choose, you need to be very cautious and very discriminating about what you tell and to whom. Much adoption-related information is private information for your child that does not need to be revealed. If, for example, you determine that it is better for your child that you inform school officials about a past history of abuse because some behavioral issues are present, you would do better to limit the amount of information that you disclose and to provide that information only to the particular teacher involved. Even though school records are supposed to be confidential, no one can guarantee that confidentiality will be maintained for your child.

6

‸‸‸

SPEAKING POSITIVELY

"The hardest part about adoption for me has been people saying 'How could you give up your child?'" explained one birthmother. "To me, accepting the fact that I wasn't able to care for my child was the important issue. Language like that implies that I was uncaring. The truth was that I tried to be especially caring, especially responsible to the needs of my child."

Language is a powerful tool that shapes societal opinion about adoption. Negative, judgmental terminology that has influenced public perception in the past reflects the assumptions that adoption is a second-best alternative, that birthparents are irresponsible and uncaring, and that adopted people are prone to troubled behaviors.

As a society, in recent years we have become alerted to the feelings of minorities and have made conscious efforts to adapt our language to avoid demeaning words and tones. It is important that we give that same respect to adopted people, birthparents, and adoptive families.

Positive Adoption Language

Positive Adoption Language, or PAL, is nonjudgmental adoption terminology that emphasizes the positive aspects of adoption as a method of family building and stresses the importance of understanding and sensitivity.

Through our own use of Positive Adoption Language and a concerted effort to educate others on its use, we can do much to change public opinion about adoption as a dignified, responsible method of family building.

Terms to Avoid	Preferred Terminology (PAL)
Real, natural parents	Birthparents, birthmother, birthfather
Real, natural children, children of your own	Biological children
Surrender, relinquish, give up for adoption, adopt out	Make an adoption plan, place for adoption
Keep the child	Choose to parent
Available children	Adoptable children
Homestudy	Parent preparation
Closed adoption	Confidential adoption
Foreign adoption	International adoption
Hard-to-place children	Waiting children
Problem children	Children with special issues, children with special challenges
Biracial, mixed	Interracial
Handicapped children	Children with disabilities
Reunion (with real parents)	Meeting with birthparents
"The child is adopted"	"The child was adopted"

Adopt-a-Talk

It seems as if everyone from clean-up crews to fundraising committees has gotten on the adoption bandwagon in quest of public sympathy and support. State transportation departments have adopt-a-highway programs aimed at roadway clean-ups, zoos have adopt-an-animal campaigns to help offset operational expenses, humane societies across the nation urge community members to adopt a pet.

The problem with these campaigns is the subtle messages that are being conveyed to adopted children. To young children, adoption is a special situation that sets some children apart from other children. Most adopted children have parents who help them understand that adoption is a special way of building a family. But when the word *adopt* is bandied about in the media and compared with raising money for zoo animals, adopted children may be confused about what they had been told is the permanence of adoption.

If adoption means a forever family, why don't we take the manatee home? Or what about Billy's family, who adopted an ostrich last year and are going to get a better animal this year? What about the Anderson family, who adopted a puppy but had to give it back when it cried all night? And Carmen, who said it was better to adopt a whale than a brother.

Certainly we, as adults, can see the fallacy of these childlike fears and the actual intent of the sponsorship programs. But, unlike small children, we are capable of thinking abstractly. This current trend of trivializing adoption in order to accomplish commercial promotions confuses children and insults all members of the adoption circle.

Is there any solution? Yes. As advocates for adopted children, we can contact program organizers and suggest alternative terminology. Manatees can be saved. Elephants can be endorsed. Highways can be helped. Rubber ducks can be sponsored. And we can all be friends, amigos, comrades, companions, or puppy pals of any worthwhile project.

Part Two

▼▲

RAISING
WELL-ADJUSTED
CHILDREN

Raising well-adjusted adopted children, so we are told, is a deceptively simple formula of strong attachments, strong family characteristics, and an effective communication style about adoption issues. Research data and the experience of adoption professionals show that the presence of these three factors prove time and again to be indicators of a successful adoptive family.

Attachments

One of the best predictors of healthy adjustment in adopted children is early emotional attachment between children and their parents. These strong attachments are easier to build when adopting infants, but it takes more than early placement. Strong attachments come from many factors, including sincere affection, good touch, empathy, listening, and understanding. They are critical components of a strong relationship, regardless of the child's age.

This issue of early adoption is very important, though. The younger the child at the time of placement, the greater the chance of a strong attachment. This is not to say that children adopted after infancy cannot develop strong attachments with their adoptive families; however, as age increases, the likelihood of strong attachment decreases. Parents who adopt older children need to work patiently and positively toward building attachments with their children. Children's advocates and adoption organizations must continue to lobby for early permanent placement for children and opportunities for pre- and post-adoption services for adoptive families.

Family Strength

Strong families have certain identifiable characteristics. They have genuine warmth and support for each other. The parents are involved in their children's schooling and activities, and family members feel happy about life in general. The children know the boundaries of behavior and the consequences when rules are broken. They see their parents as safe havens and they feel strong support from extended family members, especially the unconditional affection of their grandparents.

The result for adopted children is a strong, positive identity that comes from two factors: a feeling that they are worthwhile and a concept called *goodness of fit*, the feeling of belonging in a family. This feeling of belonging can be based on similarities of physical resemblance, values, interests, or personalities—or all of those characteristics. The stronger the similarities, the more a child feels as though she belongs. Interestingly, physical resemblance is the least important of these in measures of emotional well-being.

Communication

Effective adoption communication happens when parents have an open yet quiet form of adoption education and support for their children. In other words, the subject of adoption is always open but not always discussed. Children feel comfortable to discuss adoption with their parents because they feel that their parents are comfortable with the subject. This strength of communication also includes helping children deal with the risk factors of adoption, such as a sense of loss or disconnectedness.

Families with effective adoption communication provide security. In doing so, they achieve the goal that adoption makes no difference; that is, adoption is neither a positive nor negative force in the lives of the adopted children.

7

PREPARING FOR PLACEMENT

As soon as parents are approved for placement, their focus should shift from their own comfort about adoption issues to ensuring the comfort of the child who will enter their home. For many, this change in focus is not an overnight occurrence but a series of stages in accepting the new challenges of parenting an adopted child.

Much like a biological pregnancy that unfolds over a nine-month duration, preparing to parent a child through adoption is a psychological experience that begins when parents accept the fact that a child will join their family by adoption rather than by birth. Although almost-instant parenting may happen, predictable stages occur before placement that enable parents to move from the role of prospective adopters to adoptive parents. These steps include psychological preparation for the role change, physical and emotional preparation for the arrival of a child who has a different history and genetic background, and refocusing toward easing the child's transition.

Preparing for Your Child's Arrival

Before your child arrives, you need to learn all you can about him and the adoption issues that are likely to affect him, because many of these issues will be ongoing in your life as an adoptive family. Your child will experience grief related to adoption losses, not just once but repeatedly throughout his lifetime. If he has a learning disability, he will always suffer its effects. If he was adopted as an older child, he will always remember his life and relationships before placement. Most important, he will always be a child who needs the love and support of a permanent family.

Health Concerns

For the most part, medical care for children adopted within the United States and Canada is a matter of finding out the children's needs and transferring care and treatment. Before placement, many parents interview a number of pediatricians to determine their manner of treating children and their feelings about adoption. The practitioner can provide information about growth and development and address special concerns that prospective parents may have.

If you are adopting internationally, the medical and health information you receive may be unclear, misleading, or inaccurate, making your choice of a qualified health care provider even more important.

International adoption specialists stress the importance of locating a physician who is experienced with treating international children and who is qualified to interpret findings before placement and to diagnose and treat your child after placement. You may also have questions about health care expenses.

Successful Transitions

For children, a successful transition begins when their adoptive parents realize that children's lives do not begin the day they are adopted. Regardless of the type of adoption, children have biological relatives and genetic histories all their own.

Success in permanent placement is reflective of (1) the goodness of fit between the children and their adoptive parents, (2) the preparation of both children and family for the new situation, and (3) the availability of background information available to parents.

For a successful incorporation into a new family, older children especially need reasons for the change in their lives, and they need to feel that they are an important part of the adoption process.

A child's transition can be eased when parents do the following:

- Visit the child (or his birth country) before placement
- Send photos of the new family to the child
- Let him say good-bye to important people in his life
- Find out about his habits and preferences, especially eating and sleeping habits, and honor those preferences when possible
- Allow him to keep some transitional objects, such as photographs, toys, or articles of clothing
- Employ an interpreter if language is a barrier
- Acknowledge cultural differences, such as values, methods of discipline, or ways of showing affection
- Incorporate his birth culture into the customs of the family
- Give the child choices
- Find ways to help him understand his situation and express his feelings (provide counseling, if necessary)
- Allow him to maintain his identity (consider retaining or incorporating his given name)
- Expect that he will be influenced by his past and need time to adjust

8

^^^

BONDING AND ATTACHMENT

T
wo terms that are frequently discussed in relation to adopted children are *bonding* and *attachment.* Definitions vary for both concepts, but generally bonding is the trust that the child has in the parent—that the parent will meet the child's needs—and attachment is mutual love and affection between parent and child.

The perception among the general public is that adopted children have greater difficulty bonding and forming attachments with their parents than non-adopted children. Although some adopted children (and some non-adopted children) do have difficulty forming bonds and attachments, the incidence of actual unbonded or unattached children is low.

Most adopted children and their parents do successfully bond and attach. Children adopted after the age of six months generally need more help in bonding because they must transfer the trust or learn to trust for the first time. Attachment is built when the parents claim the children and the children feel as though they belong and fit in the family.

Bonding is established when parents consistently meet the child's needs. For parents, bonding results from an instinctive desire to protect their children. For children, bonding happens when they learn to trust that their caregivers will consistently meet their needs. That trust is later expanded to include a trust of others and of society.

Attachment develops as a mutual feeling between parent and child that the other is irreplaceable. Love is the attachment—the emotional result of bonding—and it includes positive interaction, claiming, and belonging. Attachment varies in each parent/child relationship and is influenced by personality differences, such as the level of independence or dependence between parent and child, life events, and the age and maturity of the child.

The importance of attachment lies in providing all humans with two critical elements: (1) our connections to a wide variety of people at a variety of strengths—family, friends, acquaintances, and (2) our sense of identity, that is, how we define ourselves.

Therapies exist to help create bonds and nurture attachment; however, the younger the child at placement the easier it is to build bonds and attachments. There are situations and conditions that inhibit attachments for biological as well as adopted children. Inhibitors to attachment include:

- trauma and loss,
- personality conflicts,
- negative feelings about the adoption process,
- unrealistic expectations,
- past bonds (lack of or untransferred).

Although many of these obstructions cannot be eliminated, many can be counteracted by therapies designed for children with attachment disorders.

Building Attachment

Attachment is critical in children's development. Their feelings of attachment to special people and the world around them influence their socialization, their intellectual development, and their identity formation.

In nature, the primary goal of attachment is the safe-keeping and protection of the vulnerable. People are most primed to build an attachment when they are most vulnerable. In infants, building attachments is relatively easy. With children who are adopted at an older age or who have special needs, building an attachment is easier when parents make use of those times that the children's defenses are down, when they are ill or hurt, for example. Many special-needs children have developed defense mechanisms—their learned survival behaviors—that hide their vulnerability. For the parents of those children, the task of finding vulnerable moments is more difficult.

Parents can build healthy attachments by being sensitive to their children's signals and by setting up a variety of positive encounters with their children.

Children's signals are often difficult to interpret because children do not communicate skillfully with oral language. They communicate their needs, emotions, and perceptions and misperceptions about the world through their behaviors. Adults have the responsibility of figuring out what the children are trying to communicate.

One of the secrets of successful parenting is anticipating children's needs and attempting to meet those needs before the children exhibit undesirable behaviors. This has the effect of preventing situations in which the children control the relationship. An action as simple as allowing a child to take a favorite toy to the supermarket prevents a tantrum in the store when the child wants candy in the checkout line. (When the child is successful in forcing the parent to leave the store or, worse, in getting the candy, the child becomes the controller of the situation and sets a pattern for future clashes.)

37

Another successful parenting secret is setting up a variety of positive encounters that show children how reasonable adults handle a situation. Telling a child, "Your toys are scattered across the floor, and I'm worried that someone will trip and fall over them. Please put them away neatly so we won't have to worry about someone getting hurt" shows children that differences can be resolved without conflict. When this approach is used with children who have been accustomed to different adult reactions, loud arguing, for example, the children learn other, more effective ways to get along with others. Even in a traumatic situation, such as an earthquake or flood, children can see how people work to help each other rather than allow the disintegration of the family.

Sometimes certain conditions, a personality conflict between parent and child, for example, interfere with a feeling of lovability. If you are having difficulty forming an attachment, try the following ideas for increasing your child's lovability:

1. *Validate her uniqueness and importance.* Show her by words and actions what her positive qualities are and that you believe them to be of value. Take an interest in her karate classes, for example, by attending her performances and praising the power of concentration that she is developing.

2. *Model empathy.* Listen with your heart rather than your head. Your angry child may in reality be a very frightened child.

3. *Plan times for your child to be the center of positive attention.* Plan and spend time alone together. If you find yourself making negative comments during the course of a day, make an effort to give three positive comments for each negative comment.

Attachment Difficulties

Many children with special adoption issues suffer from attachment difficulties. The nature of each child's individual situation and the prevailing attitude of social workers toward family preservation may influence the number of caregivers a child experiences—and the number of broken attachments—before the child is freed for adoption.

As human beings, we learn our sense of how people relate to each other from our initial caregivers. Parents who adopt special-needs children need to do more than build an attachment with their children. Often they need to first undo the earlier experiences and then replace those experiences with a new, healthier attachment. One technique that has been successful, for example, is preplanned interaction between parent and child that focuses on the child's positive behavior rather than reacting to negative behaviors.

9

SELF-IDENTITY AND SELF-ESTEEM

The development of self-identity and positive self-esteem is a critical part of personal development. The challenge for us all comes in knowing who we are and liking the person that we find.

For an adopted person, this question of "Who am I?" is more complex. An adopted child must find out about himself as both an adopted person and a member of his permanent family, and then somehow mesh those two identities. For some, this is an opportunity to examine two sometimes very different influences and choose what parts of those influences they would like to follow. For others, the perceived polarity between their genetic history and their environment pulls them apart and leaves them to wonder where they really fit.

As parents, we can understand that this positive identity formation is a major component in our children's successful adjustment. We sometimes struggle, though, in knowing just what the right formula is for helping our children develop that complete self.

Most mental health professionals would agree that the formula starts with self-identity—that our children need to explore their genetic influences as well as experience their adoptive family attachments. Equally important is that adoptive families value their children's genetic history and the love and caring that their birthparents had for the children no matter how inadequately the adults may have behaved.

Self-Identity

The establishment of self-identity is gradual. It begins the day we look into our mother's eyes and search for ways that we are like her. As adolescents, we identify ourselves by our friendships. As adults, we label ourselves by our relationships and achievements.

Self-identity is a question of who we really are. It involves an integration of our present self, our past self, and the person we hope to become. For adopted people who have limited knowledge of their genetic history, this self-knowledge often leaves a void that they commonly describe as a piece of themselves that is missing.

There are many ways that children can learn about their genetic heritage. The most obvious way is through contact with birth relatives. If your child was adopted at an older age, he may remember his birth relatives and their special talents and traditions. If he is involved in an open adoption situation, depending upon the degree of ongoing contact with his birth family, he can inquire about them directly or observe them firsthand.

If your child's adoption was confidential or if access to birth family members is unavailable, you can still help your child learn a great deal about his genetic heritage through books, ethnic festivals, visits to the locale in which he was born, language classes and culture camps, and friendships with other children and adults with the same background. Families should learn together and actually incorporate different customs into their own family traditions.

Self-Esteem

Self-esteem adds a value judgment to self-identity. It involves the way each individual feels about himself. Healthy, balanced self-esteem is the hallmark of a successful person. A well-adjusted person has a strong sense of who he is. He knows his strengths and his weaknesses, and he values himself as a contributing member of society.

Children who have low self-esteem are good targets for someone who wants to take advantage of them. Sexually abused children, for example, because of poor self-image are more likely to become victims again than children who have not been abused. If your child has low self-esteem, you need to actively intervene to prevent him from becoming a victim of it.

Positive self-esteem starts with three factors: (1) a secure place, (2) safe people, and (3) a feeling of belonging. One theory about building self-esteem looks at the family as a measure of how the children in that family will feel about themselves. Families with good self-esteem tend to raise children with good self-esteem. Individuals in these families feel lovable, worthwhile, capable, and responsible—and they create opportunities for other family members to feel that way, too.

Techniques for Building Self-Esteem

Do:

- Establish routines that your child can count on—regular times for eating and napping, for example.
- Encourage pride in your child's heritage. "Your skin is such a warm, beautiful color. I wonder if your Brazilian mother had such lovely skin."
- Foster a sense of belonging. "You and Daddy both enjoy fixing things for the family."
- Teach and expect your child to share and to work cooperatively.
- Set reasonable rules and consequences.
- Allow your child to experiment, to create, to make choices and mistakes, and to learn.

- Encourage your child to participate in group activities, such as sports or musical performances. Attend performances.
- Praise specific skills and behaviors. (This is especially important if you are trying to counteract behaviors that the child may feel tentative about—a birth history of neglect, for example.) Say, "You help Daddy with the baby by getting diapers when he needs them. I can tell that you really know how important it is to take care of a little baby."

Do not:

- Call your child "bad." Behaviors, not children, are bad.
- Intervene on your child's behalf in minor matters. Paving the way and righting every wrong prevent children from learning to handle situations themselves.
- Allow your child to take responsibility for adult behaviors. Children need help in understanding that they did not cause their parents to divorce, that they did not do anything to cause their birthparents to hurt them, and so on.
- Be overly critical. Try to focus on people's strengths rather than their shortcomings.
- Overdo praise. An inflated sense of self sets children up for unrealistic expectations of themselves. An attitude of self-importance can also interfere with socialization when others do not see the child in the same glowing terms.

10

~~~~~~

HELPING CHILDREN ACCEPT ADOPTION

All adopted children have difficult information to process simply because they are not living with their birthparents. This includes children in very loving situations in which the adoption was carefully planned.

Timing

Many adoption experts believe that it is better for children never to remember a time when they did not know that they were adopted. Your acceptance of adoption as a part of your child's life empowers her to develop that same sense, a sense that adoption does not matter. This does not mean you should not talk to your child about adoption. Rather it means that discussing the method in which she entered your family is an ongoing process rather than a moment of enlightenment followed by a handful of subsequent discussions during her development.

Advocates of later disclosure believe that children are not ready to understand adoption until the age of six or seven, when they have a better grasp of conception and birth. The risk that the children will learn of their adoption from a playmate is minimal, they suggest, especially when compared to the potential for confusion with too early disclosure.

Regardless of your choice of the time at which to disclose the fact of your child's adoption, most experts agree that it is critical that children learn about their adoption from their parents and that the parents present the information in an open, positive manner.

Presenting Information

Depending on your child's age and level of understanding, your conversations will center on such issues as what it means to be adopted, the retelling of her own individual adoption story, and what her birthparents' decisions and actions do and do not mean about her.

We need to help our children sort through the internal conflict that arises over the idea that, in a perfect world, children's conceivers and birthgivers are also the children's permanent caregivers, but for adopted children, this is not the case. Our own children do, however, have parents who chose to raise them and who care about them and love them. This is a loss issue for our children. It is one that we will be unable to resolve for them.

Ways to Help Your Child Accept Adoption

1. *Share your child's personal story with her.* Include the details of the day she was born (inasmuch as you know them), information about her genetic background, and any life experiences and relationships before placement.
2. *Continually reaffirm her place in the family.* Your child may have fears about leaving her adoptive family, for example. If she was told that her birthparents could not raise her because they were too young, she may deduce that when her birthparents are older, they may change their mind and decide to reclaim her. Your reaffirmation that placement is permanent will help ease her fears.
3. *Encourage her to express and share her feelings.* Once these feelings are expressed and adoption is

accepted as something that happened, your child will be able to begin to heal. For example, "I think I would feel sad if my birthparents weren't able to raise me. And I'll bet being away from you makes them feel sad, too" validates the child, the birthparents, and the true difficulty of the situation.

4. *Help her externalize responsibility for the decisions her birthparents made.* Whatever the reasons behind adoptive placement, your child needs to understand that they were not the fault of the child.

5. *Value her genetic history, ethnicity, and past relationships.* It is important to provide her with her own personal information and to expose her to friends and role models with the same heritage as she has. It is even more important that you live this acceptance of the value of other peoples by having your own friends of various ethnic and social backgrounds.

Life Histories

The usual method of conveying information about life history involves pictures, oral stories, baby books, extended family get-togethers, and so on. The same should be true for adopted children. Your child needs a permanent treasury, a record of her entry into the human race and her road to permanence. As long as efforts toward authenticity are made, it is of little significance that this record may need to be re-created.

An important and effective way for adoptive parents to help their children bridge the gap from their previous history to their adoptive home is by preparing life books and personal stories. These tangible records of the children's histories link past to present and validate the important people and events in their lives. Your child may not have a baby book; she can certainly have a life book and a personal story, which will preserve important memories before, during, and after placement.

Life Books

A life book is prepared like a scrapbook. Written in chronological order, it presents significant people and events from throughout the child's history—birth family members, foster care providers, favorite adults—as well as memorable events, such as a trip to the circus or Christmas at Grandma Irene's in Montana. Life books are particularly important for children who join their family at a later age or who have different ethnicities than their parents.

Children are usually involved in making their own books and choosing the important events to include. If photographs are available, they are included along with brief descriptions of the events or other people in the photo. When photographs are not available, some families use magazine pictures or drawings.

If your child was adopted internationally, include pictures of her country of origin. If she has a different ethnicity, include pictures of people of her culture enjoying popular customs. Older children can draw people and events as they remember them.

Young children will enjoy looking at simple pictures and hearing their parents' words as they retell the story of the children's lives. As they get older they will enjoy hearing the stories again and again, listening for more detailed accounts of their stories and asking questions about adoption and early relationships. These are important opportunities for families to be close and to share information and feelings about adoption.

Personal Stories

Creating personal stories is another useful activity that adoptive parents can enjoy with their children. These narratives, which become "The Story of (Your Child)," are factual, accurate accounts of the circumstances related to the child's birth and placement. They include information about the child and her significant relationships before placement as well as a description of her entry into the family.

Personal stories are appropriate for children adopted at all ages and through any placement situations. Their importance lies in the permanent written chronicle of the child's early life experiences and the transition to permanent placement. Later these stories may serve as references about key people, dates, and locations that may help the children complete searches or fill in gaps of missing information.

When you make a journal such as this, take care to value your child's birthparents. Give the birthparents feelings so they seem human and so your child feels a linkage with the human race. One effective technique is to include any knowledge that you have about acts of the birthparents that showed love and caring for your child.

Even if parental rights were terminated, the birthparents can be portrayed as caring people who lacked the skills to parent. If a difficult birth history is a part of your child's history, the story should still portray the birthparents as valuable people even though their behaviors may not have been wise. (Difficult conception details such as rape, incest, or attempted abortion should not be shared with preschoolers. That information is better saved until middle childhood and shared only after consulting a professional in adoption.)

However much you decide to reveal, take care that the information you present is accurate and will not be contradicted later when your child receives more information. This bears repeating. Your child's journal will become a lifeline that validates her self-worth and inclusion in the human race. You must present accurate information in a kind and sensitive manner.

Other useful techniques that help to personalize the story are including descriptions of your child's country of origin or birth culture if it differs from yours, and your own feelings and reactions to the events surrounding placement.

The Story of Keisha

Not too many years ago, a man and a woman (boy/girl or names can be inserted) made a baby. They knew that it is very important to take good care of a baby. But they knew that they were not able to take care of a baby at that time in their lives. They must have hurt inside and cried.

Then they found out about adoption and they found out that there were other people who could take good care of babies.

Mom and Dad wanted to raise a child together and we tried to make a baby, but at that time we were unable to make a baby. And we were very sad. Mommy cried and Daddy was very quiet.

Then we found out that there was another way to make a family. We talked to the adoption agency. And we learned that one way was to find a woman who could not take care of a baby. We found out that we could put an ad in the paper asking if we could help her by taking care of her baby. And then we found Sheila and Mike. They needed someone to take care of the baby that Sheila was going to have.

When you were born, Sheila's mother called to tell us that you were a beautiful baby girl with dark curly hair and big brown eyes. She said that Sheila was happy to see how pretty and nice you were.

49

Mike felt so sad that they could not care for you that he could not come to the hospital to see you. Sheila held you very tight and told you that she loved you. She felt bad when she had to leave the hospital without you. She and her friends left you little presents so you would be happy. She knew that Mom and Dad would love you and take good care of you and that you would like our family.

11

‸‸‸

DEVELOPMENTAL STAGES

The practice of a comfortable openness about adoption begins the day you bring your child home. The more comfortable you are with adoption and the related issues, the more comfortable your child will be, and the greater the likelihood of his successful adjustment.

Conversations with your child will vary depending on his developmental stage, temperament, and outside influences. If your seven year old has a friend with a stepparent and stepsiblings, for example, he will be more receptive to conversations about different ways that families are built. Lack of response to some of your well-planned conversations does not mean lack of understanding or interest, however. Your child may just need more time to process the information, or he may be quite comfortable with the topic of adoption and his role as an adopted child. At every age, however, your child needs to know that his birthparents loved him and felt bad that they were unable to care for him and that he is now an integral part of your family.

Birth to Age 2

Children adopted as infants experience a pain of separation from their original caregivers much like children who are adopted at a later age. All adopted infants must adjust to new sights, new sounds, new smells, and new experiences.

During your child's pre- and early verbal stages, you have a perfect opportunity to get comfortable with the subject of adoption around your child and to build the foundation for future discussions. These early talks should focus on his entry into the family and the related positive feelings. "We were so happy when we heard that you had been born. We couldn't wait to tell Grandma and Grandpa."

This is also a good time to get comfortable with the idea of the significant people in your child's birth history by mentioning them in your conversations with him: "You have such a pretty smile. I'll bet your birthmother (or your Colombian mother) had a pretty smile just like you." If you are more comfortable not using the term *birthmother* until the child is older, refer to her by name—"This is the blanket that Sheila made for you. She is very special and she loved you very much."

Your child, of course, will not understand these discussions, but he will become familiar with the word *adoption* and the tones you use in discussing the subject.

This is also a suitable time to begin focusing on similarities between your child and other family members so that he feels a sense of belonging. "You laugh just like your daddy. It's fun to be with you."

Ages 3 to 5

Around the age of three, children start to learn about family and develop an interest in how and when they were born. Before children can understand adoption and the different ways families are made, they need to understand how children are made.

Children around this age will begin to wonder if they grew in their mothers' tummies. This is a good opportunity to explain adoption and the different ways that children can enter their families. It is important for you to tell your child about his origins and his ancestors, not just his history after placement in your family. This total sense of a life story is critical in the development of his identity and should include whatever details you know about the day he was born. He needs to know that he was born just like all other children, that he is part of a family, and that families are made up of people who live together and love each other.

Near the age of four, children begin to wonder about their birthmothers; questions about birthfathers tend to come later. This is a good time to bring out photos, letters, or mementos from the birthparents. If you do not know the answers to your child's questions or if the story involves a difficult past, answer with "maybe" responses while affirming the value of the people involved and the difficulty of their situation before the child's placement: "I don't know what your birthmother is like. Maybe she's good at sports just like you. But I do know that she cared about you very much because she [nursed you, wrapped you in a beautiful blue blanket, took you to an orphanage so you could be cared for, and so on]."

By allowing him to think about, even fantasize about his birthparents, you assist your child in accepting his role in the family and developing a sense of positive self-esteem. His curiosities may lead to fears about such issues as the birthparents reclaiming him, though, so it is important that you check on his understanding of adoption.

Ages 6 to 8

Somewhere around the age of eight, children will become engrossed in the idea of adoption and curious about their birthparents and what life would have been like had their birthparents been able to raise them. Children at this age also question why their birthparents placed them for adoption. If the children are being raised in an open adoption situation, they may address these questions directly to the birthparents.

No matter how hard adoptive parents try, they are unable to spare their children loss and grief feelings. You can help your child deal with these difficult issues by pairing every explanation with a feeling: "I'll bet that hurts" or "If I were in your position I'd be angry." If your child requests more information that you do not have available, volunteer to find the answer: "Let's write to the agency and see if we can find out."

It is important to know for yourself and to stress to your child that, as in all situations that move children through to adoptive placement, someone cared enough about him to take the first step that resulted in placement. Reassure your child that his placement is permanent.

Ages 9 to 12

During middle childhood, children gain a deeper understanding of what adoption means. Some of the early signs of grieving may surface as the children begin problem solving, categorizing, and seeing relationships. They may begin to see the public side of adoption, that socially they are different from their friends, even though they may not understand why that difference matters.

Children at this age frequently benefit from adoption support groups and the opportunity they provide for friendships with other children who were also adopted.

Many mental health experts believe that children are better able to process difficult adoption information during middle childhood than during adolescence, when they have enough problems just being teenagers. If your child's history does include unpleasant circumstances, take care to share the facts without making a judgment. You may want to consult a mental health professional with experience in difficult adoption issues when your child is in middle childhood.

Ages 13 to 15

It is not uncommon for your young teenager to not want to be around any parents, birth or adoptive. This is a particularly difficult time for most children, who want to fit in and not be noticed for any differences whatsoever.

Being different can be especially trying for children of different ethnic or racial backgrounds from their peers. Racial prejudice may influence friendships that were acceptable as childhood relationships but not as dating relationships. Transracially or transculturally adopted teens may also have difficulty achieving acceptance from people of their own race because of differences in language, customs, or mannerisms.

In open adoptions, when children are having difficulty adjusting to adolescence, some parents have been successful in allowing their children to live with their birthparents for a specific period of time, such as a summer vacation. The reasons behind the success of this approach are unclear—the birthparents may have experienced similar difficulties in adolescence and can therefore help the children, or the children may develop a new appreciation for their parents. For children of transracial open adoptions, such a move often helps establish racial connectedness. Like visitations with a noncustodial divorced parent, these visits may help provide a balance for the children.

Ages 16 to Adult

Like all young people, adopted teenagers are trying to discover how they fit into the world at the same time that they are attempting to establish their independence. Frequently this is a period of heightened interest in adoption and in obtaining information about their birth families.

As these children develop sexually, they begin to examine the different options that their birthparents had and, frequently, judge those actions and decisions. They also struggle with achieving their own balance between the influences of genetics and environment, especially if the social status or education level of their birthparents is vastly different from that of their adoptive parents.

We can help our children deal with conflicts over the birthparents' actions and decisions by pointing out the difficulties that their birthparents may have encountered: societal attitudes about out-of-wedlock pregnancies at the time of the child's conception, the continuing stigma in many countries against children born out of wedlock, and the necessary skills related to parenting children.

Children who were a part of a confidential adoption may develop a desire to search for their birthparents at this stage. Children adopted internationally may express an interest in a homeland visit. Many mental health professionals with experience in adoption issues stress that, regardless of the children's wishes, parents should continue to be the decision-makers about family matters, including homeland visits and searches, until the children reach adulthood.

If your child is in turmoil, a search for missing birth relatives or a return to the homeland is not recommended until his issues are resolved; otherwise, he is setting himself up for the fantasy that finding this information will fix everything. Because of the difficulty of the search process and the likelihood that important records may become inaccessible, however, if you feel that your child might be interested in initiating a search you may want to begin to access information as soon as possible. You may choose not to act on leads or identifying information until later, but the information will be available for you then.

12

~~~~~~

BLENDING FAMILIES

The addition of children to any family results in a shift in family dynamics. Whether the new family members join the family through birth, adoption, or step-relationships, the security of each child is threatened. A former only child has a sibling. The only girl suddenly has to share her status—and possibly her bedroom and toys—with a new sister. The former youngest child becomes a middle child. Family dynamics become further complicated when the new additions upset the birth order of the children previously in the family. In the case of an older child adoption, for example, the former oldest child could suddenly become a middle child.

Successful harmonizing of biological and adopted children becomes a matter of blending all of the individual identities into a bonded family unit.

Blending Biological and Adopted Children

Adoption happens to families, not just to children. For immediate family and extended family members who are not involved in an adoption until after the parents have made the decision to adopt, the addition of new children can result in abrupt changes in family harmony. Everyone in the family needs to be prepared for changes in his or her own role in the family that new children bring. The greatest adjustment will need to be made by the children who are most displaced, for example, the youngest who suddenly becomes the middle child or the only girl who now has a sister. This displacement frequently results in testing behaviors.

The two most commonly expressed concerns of parents of blended families are fairness and building positive sibling relationships. These issues are similar to those that parents encounter when the family includes stepchildren. In any blended family, rearrangement of birth order status or attention that is focused on a particular child can cause internal strife in the family.

Myths about Blended Families

Societal assumptions about adoption can interfere with parents feeling comfortable about fairness issues and the strength of sibling relationships within their blended families. Not only do many people believe these myths about adoption and adoptive families, they commonly voice them aloud, often within earshot of children.

These perceptions can be very powerful. They can subtly influence the way that parents treat both their adopted and their biological children. One mistake that parents of blended families make, for example, is to try to minimize the birthing experience so that adopted children do not feel as though they have lost out on something. Another common mistake is for parents to overreact to sibling rivalry, especially when adoption issues are used as weapons.

Families do not need to shield their adopted children from insensitive remarks as much as they need to reaffirm the children's place in the family through their responses to such remarks. Comments such as "Aren't you happy now that you (are going to) have your own, real child?" spoken in the presence of the adopted children are, unfortunately, not uncommon. A response from the parents that is directed to the children, for example, "She must not realize how it feels in our family that we all love each other," addresses the comment while reinforcing the children's place in the family.

It is important to foster acceptance of differences among all people and to talk with your biological and adopted children about differences, especially if there are racial differences or special-needs issues in the family. Your children will be asked questions when you are not there, and if you have addressed these issues as a family, they will be better prepared to field probing questions.

When speaking with your children about differences, start by validating their feelings: "I'll bet it makes you feel sad when the kids at school make fun of Sonia." Then identify choices that the children have: "You could ignore them, tell them that you don't want to play with people who are prejudiced, or tell them that your parents say that people who behave like that are ignorant. Or if you like, I can speak to the teacher about their behavior." Finally, practice responses with your children: "I'd rather be with someone who likes all kinds of people" is a response that children can use.

Sense of Fairness

Parents often struggle a great deal with trying to equalize life between their biological and adopted children. This activity is both exhausting and counterproductive. Children's circumstances are never equal and never need to be equalized regardless of the method in which they entered the family. Children do not need to be treated equally—in fact, it reinforces their desire to keep score and conveys the message that identical treatment means equal amounts of love.

Instead, parents need to give to each child based on what that child needs. A healthy blended family is one that can celebrate each individual's unique situation. Treating children fairly does not mean treating them equally.

Attempts to equalize treatment by favoring adopted children teach the children to become victims of their adoption.

A better course of action is to prepare the children to handle life's inequities and to cope with its realities.

The goal for blended families should be to celebrate all the different ways the children entered the family. Valuing and celebrating each child's story prevents one situation from being minimized to compensate for another. A slightly different but similarly counterproductive version involves parents overemphasizing the "specialness" of adopted children.

Sibling Relationships

Children who share the experience of growing up together are siblings, regardless of the way that the children enter the family. The process of forming strong sibling relationships is the same for children who are raised in families formed by birth or adoption. (This is not so true for adoptions of older children who already have knowledge of other siblings.)

Sibling relationships help children establish their self-identity. They are a safe arena for children to gain experience in handling all kinds of interpersonal relationships, including competition, aggression, conflict resolution, and cooperation. Life with siblings is a child's first cooperative living experience. It presents an opportunity to develop close, intimate relationships with someone other than the parents.

Sibling rivalry, a part of nearly all sibling relationships, is frequently identified by parents as one of the most difficult elements of child-rearing. One minor source of relief for parents may be the realization that sibling rivalry is common and a normal part of child development.

This rivalry may be very intense in a blended family, especially if some children are the objects of excessive attention. Children who are visibly different—children of interracial heritage may be particularly striking, for example—

may draw attention away from other children in the family. Some adopted children may receive gifts from their birth relatives in excess of what their siblings receive on their birthdays. All sorts of situations can happen that result in problems with jealousy or self-esteem.

A new child's arrival in a family is a significant event in itself. New family members, regardless of the newly restructured birth order, are likely to draw attention away from the other children in the family. The challenge for the children already in the family may be a struggle just to continue to fit in.

You will probably be surprised at how creative and adaptive your children become in the heat of sibling rivalry. You can expect that they will use the information about how they entered the family as ammunition during conflicts. You will be as likely to hear "You always do more for her because she's adopted" as the opposite response of "You care more about him because he's your real son." You will be equally surprised to hear your children jump to one another's defense, especially when one is the object of taunts or prejudice.

An additional source of sibling conflict may occur when adopted children express an interest in searching. Biological children can feel threatened by the fear of losing their siblings, a fear that they may express as "Wasn't our family good enough?" An ideal solution is family communication and sharing in the search.

13

▼▲

SCHOOL ISSUES

E nrollment in school can bring forth a whole new set of issues for adopted children. Some of these issues— confusion about completing family tree assignments, for example—are fairly predictable for all adopted children. Others may be normal, predictable issues for a smaller number of adopted children—language or acculturation challenges for those adopted as older international children, for example. There are also unpredictable problems that may not show up until children enroll in school. Examples of these include certain learning disabilities, some mental retardations, and various health or behavior disorders.

When difficulties do arise, parents may need to advocate aggressively for their children in order to convince school systems to provide appropriate services that they are legally required to provide.

Enrollment

Some parents, particularly parents of newly arrived international children, may question the advisability of immediate enrollment versus temporary postponement of schooling in order to obtain specialized assistance in such areas as language or cultural acclimation.

For the most part, the answer to that question is that the job of children is to be in school. Parents need not expect children to understand the language or to perform well academically. They need only expect that the children attend school. This expectation holds true whether the children have arrived with only three weeks of school left before summer vacation or have never attended school before. Postponing education presents the incorrect message that children do not have to attend school and sets the children up for trauma when eventually they are forced to attend.

Appropriate Placement

The vast majority of children, adopted or non-adopted, function well in the public school system. There are other students, though, whose needs cannot be met satisfactorily through traditional public education.

If you think traditional public schooling is not an appropriate choice, you may want to consider alternatives right from the start rather than waiting until the public school has failed for your child. Options to traditional public schooling include home schooling, home-bound schooling, private or parochial schools, or alternative schools within the public school system. These alternatives can be part of the child's long-term educational plan, or they can be used to provide more individualized attention or a transition into the public school system.

Even if you decide the public school system is appropriate for your child, there are other issues that may surface. If your child is of indeterminate age or has lived on the streets with experiences far different than those of a normal six year old, for example, you will need to make some decisions about grade-level placement.

When making decisions about grade-level placement, consider not only the current school year but also future school years in the event that your child makes some dramatic changes over the course of the year. A small child of unknown age may seem appropriately placed in second grade. However, during the course of the year he may grow dramatically and enter puberty, making the second-grade placement inappropriate.

Parents can use medical professionals to assist them in making placement decisions, but they also need to be aware that at some time in the future, changes, including a double or triple promotion, may be in order.

At the other end of the spectrum are children who have grown up in an orphanage without ever having had the opportunity to make an independent decision. For those children, grade-level placement based on chronological age may be too ambitious.

Regardless of the special needs that your child brings to the educational system, you need to actively plan and participate in his education in order for his experience to be successful. This includes visiting the school and teachers, attending school programs, educating yourself about services to which your child is legally entitled, and, in many instances, being an aggressive advocate for your child.

Predictable Difficulties

Certain areas of the school experience may present difficulties for adopted children. Generally these obstacles are related to the structure of the school environment, individual differences in learning styles, and the school curriculum.

Although attempts are made to adapt to the changing needs of students and the changing expectations of school systems, most classrooms continue to be operated rather traditionally. Children who were adopted at a later age may have difficulty adapting to the rather rigid structure common in most public schools. The behaviors of these children are often interpreted as oppositional when, in fact, the behaviors may express grief for the abrupt loss of significant individuals or the child's attempts to take back control of his environment.

Adopted children also seem to be at greater risk for certain learning disabilities and biological conditions. Whatever the actual cause associated with this higher risk, these disabilities do affect the ways that children learn. Generally the public school system does not easily accommodate a wide variety of disabilities or learning styles.

The third area of schooling that can present difficulties for adopted children is curricular. As an example, a common middle-grades activity is the family tree assignment, in which children place the names of their genetic relatives on branches of the tree. A similarly troublesome assignment occurs again in high school biology, when students study genetic influences on physical traits—eye color, for example. Obviously the issue is not children's reluctance to learn about genetic influences; the issue is the children's right to keep their genetic backgrounds private.

Another curricular problem that adopted children encounter relates to stereotypical expectations based on race. Children of Native American descent may be expected to report on a new perspective on the settling of the Old West. Textbooks may depict people of Middle Eastern descent as terrorists. Children of Asian heritage may be expected to excel academically, regardless of their individual abilities. For adopted children, such situations bring forth issues that may be sensitive and that are, at the very least, personal matters.

Frequently the effects of these obstacles can be offset by communication between the parent and the school. Adoptive parents may wish to initiate special culture days at the local elementary school and help teachers incorporate lessons about the contributions and customs of people of various cultures. Local adoptive-parent support groups generally know which teachers assign family trees and can suggest ideas for helping adopted children complete the assignment. Sometimes parents must intervene on behalf of their children and request alternative assignments or special services.

Additional Difficulties

Beyond the normal adoption-related issues, entry into the public school system can bring about certain issues that do not present major problems outside of the school setting. Children who were raised in an inner city may be able to communicate well until they enter a suburban school system and learn that their use of the English language is not acceptable. Exceptionally large or exceptionally small children can function perfectly well until they enter a school environment in which their size identifies them as being very different from the norm. Other issues, such as acculturation or lack of education, may present problems when children enter school. These are relatively minor issues that only marginally affect children outside the school setting.

There are other issues that present major problems for children both in the school setting and outside of school. These issues may or may not have been evident before the children's entry into school but, once apparent, significantly affect the children's life in both settings. They include attention deficit disorder, prenatal drug or alcohol exposure, learning disabilities, physical impairments, mental retardation, behavior disorders, and certain health concerns.

When Problems Arise

Sooner or later you may get a call from the school notifying you that your child is not doing well. When this happens, you need to remember that educating children—including your child—is the job of the school system.

When problems arise, your first step should be to go in and ask the school officials what they plan to offer for your child. Whatever the cause of the problems, it is their responsibility to come up with a solution. If their solution seems to fall short or is inappropriate, suggest an alternative. Remember that no public school system can refuse any child for any reason. They must educate your child.

The best outcomes result from a home-school partnership. Regardless of the expertise that school personnel provide, you are the expert on your child. The background information that you have on your child, his behaviors outside of school, and your own intuition are strong factors in determining his educational needs.

14

WHEN PEOPLE ASK ABOUT ADOPTION

S ociety has a difficult time dealing with adoption in general. Add to that adoptive families who are noticeably different than the norm—transracial families, families whose children have physical or emotional challenges, or families parented by singles or same-sex couples, for instance—and even well-meaning people are often confused and tend to speak or act inappropriately.

Many of these people are well-meaning but uneducated about adoption. Perhaps many of us behaved that way in our pre-adoption lives. What cannot be overlooked are people whose questions and comments convey negative intent, such as prejudice about adoption or adopted children. Regardless of the questioner's intent, our answers must convey our children's belongingness in our families.

Inappropriate Questions
Adoptive parents need to be aware that people who are in the habit of commenting on differences may be prone to racism and other forms of prejudice. Others may need to feel superior, and some just simply do not know any better.

A lot of questions and challenges also come from the playground. Best friends are as likely to be cruel as the neighborhood bully. Close friends may try to figure out for themselves what is happening, and look for faults in the adopted child to reassure themselves that the same thing will not happen to them—for example, "Your parents couldn't keep you because you stutter."

Other children are frightened of the concept of adoption; their parents may tell them that "Amy's mother couldn't keep her." What the children hear is that sometimes children do not stay with their parents. They develop a fear that they themselves will lose their own parents and never see them again.

What is important is that every time someone questions your child's belongingness or her origins, you need to tie the child back to the family with the same statement: "She's like her father, she's (tall, quiet, smart, friendly, and so on)." This is important to maintain your sense of family even when your child is a teenager and embarrassed by the situation. Your job is your family, not public relations for adoption.

Proactive Responses

When you have a mind-set about adoption that focuses on affirming the role of your child in the family, you will have an easier time responding to questions that come your way. Your mind-set can be built from your response to these questions:

- Do I want to discuss this information with anyone?
- Do I want to discuss this information with this person?
- Do I want to discuss this here?
- Is this an appropriate time?

If you are in the supermarket with your child, maybe you do not want to detract from your time together to answer questions about adoption. You can even respond aloud by saying to your child, "Do you want to answer that question? Is this the right place?"

As a rule, parents should never give out information that they have not shared with their children. The decision to share information about the children's birthparents or the reasons for adoption rightfully belong to the children. Parents of babies or young children can deflect inquisitive questions with "We plan to let her decide how she wants to answer that question. You can ask her when she's twelve."

If you do get caught off guard and find yourself in an adoption discussion that you deem inappropriate, try one of these three devices: humor, deflecting the question ("Why would you be interested in that question?"), or deferring information ("Please call me at home and I will be happy to discuss adoption issues with you").

Empowering Children

Children need empowerment to handle questions about their adoptive status. Questions will typically come up at school, and children need strategies that let them preserve their privacy while dealing with the intrusions.

One way in which children learn how to respond is by listening to how their parents respond. When you are asked an unsuitable question about your child or about adoption, give strangers the answers that you want your child to hear, regardless of the question that was actually presented.

Practicing answers also makes spontaneous answers easier for children. A response such as "Why do you want to know?" helps children retain the balance of power by buying time to think of an appropriate response and to determine the questioner's intent.

Children need to know also that it would be impossible to have a handy answer ready for every probing question about adoption. Sometimes they will get caught off guard and suffer an assault for which they have no response.

If your child does experience a particularly brutal assault, you need to help her cope with the aftermath. Start

by validating her feelings about the inappropriate question—
"I'll bet it hurt when he said that." Then ask your child how
you can help and follow her lead. You may decide that
informing the school or calling the offensive child's parents
is an action to employ. That action takes empowerment away
from your child, however, since you as the parent become
the person who handles the situation rather than the child.
Often the best protection you can offer your child is teaching
her how to respond herself while you stand back and provide
a watchful eye.

Hints for Empowering Children

1. *Validation.* "I'll bet that made you feel bad. I know
   that's hard."
2. *Exploration.* "How would you like to handle this?"
   This implies that you believe the child can handle it
   even if she thinks she cannot.
3. *Counsel.* "Let's spend a few days figuring out some
   responses that you might be able to use."
4. *Intervention, if suitable.* It may be appropriate to
   contact the school or the other child's parents.

Sample Answers to Probing Questions to Children

Q. Are those your real parents?

A. Yes.

Q. How come you don't look like your parents?

A. They are older than I am.

Q. Didn't your other parents love you?

A. Yes.

Q. Then why did they give you away?

A. Why do you want to know?

71

Q. Where did you get that red hair? long legs? slanted eyes?

A. From my mom and my dad.

Sample Answers to Probing Questions to Parents

Q. Is she yours?

A. Yes.

Q. Are they sisters?

A. Yes (the answer is the same whether or not the children are biologically related).

Q. What were her "real" parents like?

A. Well, I'm 38 years old, 5′2″ and on the slim side, and so on.

Q. Didn't her birthmother care about her?

A. Yes, she cared about her very much.

Q. Why did they give her up for adoption?

A. Birthparents choose to make an adoption plan for many reasons. If you are interested in learning more about adoption, call me at home.

Q. Where did that kinky hair (or those blue eyes, or any other differentiating physical trait) come from?

A. It is genetic.

Q. Does she have any brothers and sisters?

A. (Your answer depends on the number of siblings in your family, or if the child has contact with her genetic relatives, the number of siblings that she claims.)

Q. What if you get pregnant now?

A. We would be excited for Susan to have a brother or sister.

Q. What if her parents change their mind?

A. What would we change our minds about?

Q. How much do her birthparents know about you?

A. Why could that question possibly interest you?

Q. When will you tell her that she was adopted?

Q. What will you tell her about her "other" parents?

Q. Will you help her locate her birthparents?

Q. How much did the adoption cost?

A. If you are interested in learning more about adoption, call me at home and I can give you the number of a good adoption agency.

Remember that you do not have to answer any question about adoption. Period. The questioner has invaded your child's privacy by inquiring. You do not need to be open. You do not need to be sensitive in your response. All you need to do is consider the feelings of your child.

Sometimes it helps to have a pat response ready, such as "We only discuss family issues with people who have shown us their financial statements." Children can also have a non-response ready. "So?" can counter practically every question that might be presented by other children. If you practice pat responses yourself and with your child, you will have equipped yourselves to defuse the effects of a great many probing questions.

Part Three

‸‸

ISSUES FOR YOUR CHILD

Adoptions are generally defined by the type of adoptable child and the degree of confidentiality built into the adoption plan. Adoptable children may be babies born in the United States, transracially adopted children, international children, or older children. Many children fit into more than one category—a child from Colombia adopted as an eight year old by Caucasian parents, for example. The adoption design may be confidential or open, or it may contain features of both.

Each of these adoption types has different but fairly predictable effects on children and their families. They can provide valuable clues to the challenges that children face and to appropriate parenting techniques.

Adoption Characteristics

The tens of thousands of children who are adopted every year represent a cross section of global society. Although children may fit multiple descriptions, the groupings serve to clarify common issues. The issues for a child who is racially different from her family, for example, will be different than for a child who is racially similar. A child who was adopted at an older age will have separate issues from a child adopted as an infant.

Modern adoptions also cross a broad spectrum of confidentiality issues—from a completely *confidential adoption,* in which no identifying information is available, to a completely *open adoption*, an arrangement that includes full disclosure of identifying information between birth and adoptive parents and an agreement to maintain ongoing direct contact for the benefit of the child.

Only a small percentage of contemporary adoptions are at either end of the spectrum, however. Adoptions tend toward confidentiality or openness depending on the wishes of the birth and adoptive parents and the needs of the children, but most do not embrace either extreme completely.

A popular alternative is *semi-open adoption*, a plan that involves the sharing of information through an intermediary. A semi-open plan has some of the features of a confidential adoption and some of the features of an open adoption. Some plans will lean toward greater confidentiality; others will lean more toward openness.

15

BABIES BORN IN THE
UNITED STATES

I n spite of current publicity to the contrary, healthy
babies born in the United States who are the same race
as their adoptive parents make up a significant percentage of modern adoptions.

This type of adoption is generally considered to be the
one that puts the least stress on children and presents the
greatest likelihood of success. It is true that adopted children
who are physically and emotionally healthy, who are racially
similar to their parents, who have not experienced stresses in
early life, and who have an opportunity for early bonding
have a greater likelihood of balanced adjustment to life. But
such a profile is as much a success indicator for children
raised by biological parents as it is for adopted children. (The
adoption of babies with serious emotional or physical disorders presents its own parenting challenges, which com-
pound—and in many cases supersede—the adoption issues.)

Despite the lack of conspicuous adoption differences
for healthy babies, there are, in fact, definite adoption issues
that affect these children—issues related to identity, loss, isolation, and prejudice against the social minority of adopted
persons.

Invisible Adoption

Healthy American-born children who are the same race
as their adoptive parents and who are adopted as infants risk

the status of an invisible, and potentially deniable, adoption. Children who look like their families and who have not experienced early life trauma can be absorbed into their new families without differentiation of their status as adopted persons. In fact, this was the goal for adoptive families for the greater part of this century.

While parents of children with apparent differences are forced to confront their children's adoptive status early on, parents of racially similar children adopted as babies face the temptation to hide their children's adoptive status even from the children. If they do discuss these issues with their children, they may be accused of overemphasizing the fact of the adoption, especially by extended-family members who hope to deny the differences.

A desire to maintain a sense of family normalcy, paired with a desire to protect children from the stigma of adoption, is normal and understandable. But when these desires interfere with sensitivity to the children's losses through adoption or with helping them establish an identity that includes consideration of their genetic legacy, the children are the ones who suffer.

Subtle Bias

At first thought, it would seem as though parents of racially similar children would not need to concern themselves with developing any special personal and family attitude against bias toward minorities. Caucasian parents and their children enjoy a favored status in America. Racial and cultural minorities have their own internal systems of dealing with stereotyping and prejudice. None of those groups, it would seem, would need to sensitize themselves to any additional bias from society when racially similar children are added to their families.

Although racial prejudice is the most widespread bias in this country, biases toward other minorities—including adopted persons—exist within ethnic groups, within families, and within individuals. Your adopted child will be the object of bias based on his minority status as an adopted person.

Many adoptive parents, particularly Caucasians, are not prepared for the prejudice that adopted children will face. The bias will be less obvious than outright bigotry. It may even be masked in sincerity. Nonetheless, cruel bias exists, and you will notice it early on when you hear derogatory comments about reasons for adoption, expectations of adopted children, and the motives of birthparents.

Adoptive parents are often shocked when they first hear comments such as "What a lovely child. I'm sure you'll be able to love him as much as one of your own," or "I guess his real mother didn't really care about him. Isn't he lucky to have found a family who will."

As important as it is for parents who adopt transracially or transculturally to learn to combat bias, parents of racially similar children should expect to encounter bias, too. They must learn techniques for combating it, and they must teach these techniques to their children.

Challenging Bias

Prejudice against adoption is based on stereotypical assumptions that are extended to include all members of a group of people. Bias against adoption tends to be more subtle than racial prejudice, however, and it is almost always verbal.

Covert bias is difficult to recognize. People who make biased statements tend to downplay the significance of a particular comment or dismiss the suggestion of impropriety. They may defuse the issue by implying that parents who challenge the comments are oversensitive.

Recognizing and combating bias can be especially diffi-cult when the bias comes from a close relative or an educa-tional or medical professional. The bias may be masked as a fact relevant to adoption—a grandparent suggesting weaker ties between siblings by adoption than through birth, for example.

As adults who were brought up to respect authority, we are frequently reluctant to challenge such remarks. It is easi-er to rationalize the speaker's intent (to "consider the source") or assume that the speaker has more sophisticated knowledge about the subject than we do and, therefore, is correct in his assessment.

The coping mechanism of many adults is to ignore bias, especially if it seems relatively harmless or if the speaker's intent can somehow be justified. Regardless of the intent or expertise of the source—or our own fear of making a scene and drawing even more attention to the child—we must chal-lenge biased remarks. For the sake of our children and their feelings of acceptance and value, we must take a definite, public stand against all forms of prejudice—even when our public stance makes our teenagers cringe.

Effectively combating the bias once it has been recog-nized is the second challenge for parents. What do we say, for instance, when Grandpa says, "Of course, they won't be as close as if they were *real* brothers and sisters." One response would be to say, "The experience of being adopted doesn't weaken the children's relationship with each other. They are all part of one family, and that's how we love and care about each other."

Most people who make inappropriate comments about adoption do not intend to be hurtful. They are frequently just using outdated terminology or parroting commonly held perceptions. Every encounter, therefore, does not call for a war of words about the merits of adoption. Since most biased remarks are based on misinformation, educational approaches are frequently effective.

Techniques for Counteracting Adoption Bias

1. *Use Positive Adoption Language.* Sometimes people do not know how to talk about adoption. When they hear you being comfortable with the language of adoption, they may be relieved to learn the acceptable terminology.
2. *React nonjudgmentally.* Society expects fear and suspicion between birth and adoptive parents. Statements such as "You're right. No woman could place a child for adoption—unless she felt in her heart that she was making the best, most caring decision for the welfare of her child" or "Most birthparents lose their parental rights for poor parenting skills rather than a lack of caring about their children" clearly and unemotionally explain the truths behind adoption.
3. *Explain the effects of inappropriate remarks.* Say "Ms. Smith, when you introduce Joey as being adopted you set him apart as being different. I think I'd feel second-class if I were introduced that way. I know you'd never want to hurt him. Why don't you treat him like any of your other students."
4. *Present research findings.* Tell the speaker "Yes, there may be a greater percentage of adopted children who receive mental health services. Those needs may be what brought those children into care and eventually into permanent adoptive placement. Adoption is an attempt at a solution rather than a cause."

5. *Offer to provide additional information.* Although the speaker may not be at all interested in learning more about adoption, your offer to provide information establishes that there is more to adoption than societal misperceptions, that scientific data are available that dismiss unfounded beliefs, and that you will not let bias go unchallenged. If nothing else, the speaker will learn not to make derogatory statements within your earshot.

Regardless of which techniques you employ, what is important is that you take a public stand that values all people and reaffirms your child's place in the family. Your child will learn from observing your techniques.

Issues for Children

Even if your child has a strong physical resemblance to other family members and has had the advantage of an early bonding experience, he will still be subject to the losses of adoption. Parents can be most helpful by being sensitive to these losses, communicating openly about adoption to their children, and valuing their children's birth heritage.

16

TRANSRACIALLY
ADOPTED CHILDREN

Most transracial adoptions within the United States involve African-American or interracial children adopted by Caucasian parents. The adoption of interracial children by African-American and other parents of color is common, but relatively *uncommon* are transracial adoptions of Caucasian or Native American children.

There are many similarities between raising children who were adopted transracially within the United States and raising internationally adopted children, many of whom are also racially different. Since the physical differences between the children and their parents are apparent and because race continues to be a divisive issue in America, these become key factors in both types of adoption.

The greatest difficulty for parents raising children adopted transracially arises when white parents raise non-white, especially black, children. Because of the elevated status of Caucasian people in America, not only are white parents unaccustomed to dealing with prejudice and its subtleties and, therefore, unequipped to help their minority children, they often mistakenly believe that because they themselves may be color-blind, the rest of American society is also. Minority parents who adopt transracially have the advantage of a more realistic picture of racism in America.

It is important to note also that there is a difference between race and ethnicity. A child may be black by race but Eastern European or Cuban by ethnicity, for example. For a Native American, tribal ethnicity determines customs and traditions much more than race does.

Parents who adopt transracially need to provide information and exposure to the children's racial background and ethnic heritage. For the children, developing a sense of ethnic identity in a racially dissimilar environment can become a major challenge. The children may feel alienated based on the differentness of their physical features. They will most certainly experience prejudice based on their status as members of a racial minority and the social minority of adoption. They may feel lost, without a true connectedness to their birth culture or their adopted culture.

The preeminent challenge in raising children of a different race is teaching them to combat racial prejudice while building a strong sense of self-worth. Since race is such a defining characteristic in America, in order to raise any racially different children, parents need assistance. The experience of growing up racially different in America is especially difficult for white parents to comprehend, and those who adopt transracially should make a sustained effort to understand what the children will encounter outside the home and help them deal with it.

Most transracially adopted children encounter blatant prejudice in the form of name-calling and stereotyping. Taunts may come from the racial majority who view the children's race as inferior or they may come from members of the children's own race who may accuse them of disloyalty in not acting their race. A few transracially adopted children experience more vicious and occasionally violent expressions of racism or nationalism.

Establishing Racial Identity

There is little question that racial prejudice continues in our society, even if today it tends not to be expressed verbally. Body language, voice tone, facial expression, and space and distance between people present nonverbal negative messages for people of color in a primarily white society.

The impact of racial stereotyping and prejudice on children develops gradually. By age four, children see racial differences. Children do not start thinking abstractly, though, until about age seven. Through exposure to negative racial images, children understand that there are groups who receive favorable treatment and groups who receive less favorable treatment, and that the difference is based on skin color. For children of color, these perceptions quickly transfer to negative images about themselves. By adolescence, the children can challenge these images for themselves, but before then the children are bombarded with negative images that they are powerless to deflect.

Building a strong racial identity is a two-part process based on developing strong self-esteem and a sense of pride in ethnic heritage. The process of developing a positive sense of self is important for everyone. For adopted people it can be especially challenging. For minorities in a race-conscious society, the task can be overwhelming. Transracially adopted children must feel good about themselves, and they must do that despite both subtle and blatant messages that tell them to do otherwise. The task for parents is to help their children develop a strong sense of themselves while combating the effects of racism and racial stereotypes.

Counteracting Stereotypes

Children will develop a sixth sense about prejudice based on their own experiences, perceptions that parents may have to work hard to notice—slow service from waiters or suspicious looks from shopkeepers, for example.

It is possible, and advisable, for parents to attempt to counteract the deluge of racial stereotypes that invade their children's lives. You can start by understanding where your child is developmentally and providing different, positive images. These should include a cross section of printed and visual media and real people: books showing minorities working in a variety of occupations, friendships with people with different ethnic backgrounds, and so on.

Preparing for Racism

Parents of transracially adopted children need to prepare their children for racism ahead of time rather than waiting until the children encounter taunts or racial epithets. This preparation involves telling the children what to expect and giving them the tools to combat the teasing when it does occur. Strong self-esteem and racial identity are not enough. Children need to be prepared to encounter racism and, most important, they need effective tools and techniques to combat it.

Helping Your Child Prepare for Racism

1. *Prepare your child to be the object of racism.* Start by explaining to your child that, because of her status as a racial or ethnic minority raised in a transracial family, she can expect prejudice both from members of the racial majority and, in some instances, from members of her own ethnic group. Mention that prejudice may come in the form of name calling, racial slurs, inferior treatment, exclusion, preconceived expectations, or physical violence.

2. *Identify the names that she can expect to be called.* Explain the history behind the particular slur.

3. *Emphasize that such things do happen and they hurt.*
4. *Explain to your child that she does not deserve the treatment and that she is a good person just as she is.* Mention that people who act this way really do not know her and therefore have no right to comment on what type of person she is.
5. *Help her develop coping techniques.* Teach her problem-solving skills, including non-responses (ignoring the speaker) and verbal and nonverbal responses. Your goal is to empower your child to gain control of the situation. Responses such as staring at the speaker's clothing (especially around the torso), whispering a response, or quoting an authority figure ("My mother says that people who say that are ignorant") are all effective techniques. Practice these responses with your child and model them yourself when she is at your side.

When racism does occur, help your child through the immediate situation. Ask her what she would like you to do to help, if anything, and then follow her lead. It is important to validate her feelings about the incident. Do not try to justify the speaker's intent, since the actual intent has no bearing on how your child feels. Regardless of what the speaker actually meant or whether or not she realized what she was saying, how your child felt about it is what is important.

Discuss your child's immediate response to the situation and alternative reactions that she could have employed. If she thinks a different reaction would have been more appropriate, help her practice alternatives. If the racist act involves adults or an institution, such as the school, however, you must take direct and decisive action yourself.

Studies have shown that children adopted transracially do as well as children in same-race adoptions when parents are aware of the issues that the children face. But do not be lulled into complacency. Racism does exist, and any child of a racial minority will be the object of racism whether or not she is reporting incidents to you.

As parents of transracially adopted children, we must tell our children that racial issues are inherent in our society, help them to understand the myths and stereotypes that exist, teach them to handle subtle and overt racism, and empower them to go out in the world and deal with whatever they encounter.

Raising Children Transracially

Common Mistakes Parents Make	*Ways to Help Your Child*
Deny that racism exists	Talk as a family about racism in society; prepare your child in advance to encounter racism
Believe that love conquers all	Empower your child to combat racism
Avoid teaching coping skills for fear of bringing up unpleasant facts about society	Build a foundation of support and structure for your child by teaching how your family interacts with others
Celebrate your child's culture but not others	Celebrate many cultures; incorporate symbols of diversity in the home; develop your own friendships with diverse peoples
Ignore cultural differences	Teach your child about her heritage; instill a sense of pride in her heritage; encourage her to interact with children and adults of her cultural background
Focus on differences rather than similarities between parent and child	Recognize differences but emphasize similarities between all people
Deny an incident of racism	Trust your child's feelings that the incident occurred

Let pass a racial slur if it is not directed at your child	Deal immediately and directly with any remark that degrades on the basis of minority status
Rescue a child during an act of racism	Allow your child to handle the situation (unless the act involves an adult, at which point you must intercede)
Act powerless	Act confident; advocate for your child, especially when the incident involves adults or an institution
Lower your standards of behavior based on your perception of the child's cultural background	Maintain a good, consistent parenting style and method of discipline

17

▲▼

INTERNATIONAL CHILDREN

L ike children adopted transracially within the United States, most internationally adopted children are racially and ethnically different from their adoptive families. Both groups of children must deal with stereotypical expectations and the issues of racism and racial and ethnic identity. Children adopted internationally may face the additional difficulties of language barriers, a greater likelihood of incomplete background information and substandard medical care, and, for many, a history of institutional living.

Internationally adopted children who are ethnically but not racially different from their adoptive families—a child from an Eastern European country adopted by a Caucasian American family, for instance—will face some of the issues of children adopted in the United States who are racially similar to their parents, and some of the issues of internationally adopted children. That is, their physical features may not set them apart as different, but their need for cultural identity and connectedness to their homeland will be important issues.

Children who are adopted internationally come into care for the same reasons as children in America. These children can also have the same risk issues as children who are adopted in the United States.

Despite the seemingly uphill road that internationally adopted children may face, the majority of these children adjust and adapt very well and form strong bonds with their adoptive families and their new country.

Identity Development

Achieving balance between birth heritage and adopted heritage is one of the most crucial components of successful adaptation for internationally adopted people.

Families who complete an intercultural adoption must realize that when they adopt internationally they take on the identity of an intercultural family. Successful intercultural families incorporate part of the identity of the children and part of the identity of the parents.

For transracially or transculturally adopted children, balance comes in learning about the heritage of both the birth and the adoptive families. When specific background information is unavailable, families can pursue *cultural openness*, a process that encourages the exploration of the children's cultural rather than biological roots and the sharing of personal friendships with others of a similar background.

In many cultures outside the United States, a birth name is the mark of a person's true identity. Parents of internationally adopted children need to consider all the ramifications of a name change, especially for an older child. For children who may feel that their parents have provided everything else in life, their birth name is something that belongs solely to them rather than something that has been given by their parents. (If you have your heart set on a certain name or if your child's birth name is such that it would cause undesirable responses, try incorporating his birth name and a new name, possibly using one as a middle name, as symbolic of the blending of his two heritages.)

Health Concerns

The health of newly arrived international children is a very specialized area of pediatric medicine. Various countries, especially those with low socioeconomic conditions, have their own specific health risks—a high incidence of parasites or contagious diseases, for example.

Depending on the sophistication of the health care services in a particular country, the information that parents receive upon referral is likely to be incomplete and possibly misleading. Specialists in international adoptions recommend examinations by American pediatricians and laboratories experienced with assessing and treating international children. Even if testing was reported to have been done in the home country, it should be repeated here because of the potential for inaccuracy or exposure to disease before placement.

Common problems include exposure to tuberculosis, hepatitis B, syphilis, and intestinal parasites. HIV is currently relatively uncommon in internationally adopted children; however, the incidence of HIV exposure is expected to increase dramatically in the future.

Growth and Development

The growth and development of internationally adopted children is strongly influenced by the fact that the majority of the children have spent time in institutional care.

The longer children are in an environment such as an orphanage that lacks proper nutrition and stimulation, the more their growth will be impaired—by as much as two to three years. Other factors that influence normal growth include prenatal nutrition, ethnicity, prematurity, and the quality of early life care and experiences.

91

Orphanages also have a tremendous delaying impact on the development of children. Speech, social interaction, and play skills are greatly altered, especially if the institution is one that does not provide very much individual attention. Children can catch up rapidly, however, especially when they are placed in a nurturing environment.

Common post-arrival problems for internationally adopted children include the psychological scars of institutional living, short-term developmental delays, sensory impairment as a result of life in a sheltered environment, certain behavior problems, and sleeping problems. One of the most extreme problems that occurs is severe attachment disorder.

In general, the longer children are in institutional care, the greater the likelihood of significant problems; however, this is also an issue of resilience. Children react differently. What is overwhelming to one child may be an accepted part of life to another.

Easing the Transition to Permanence

Parents need to take great care in easing their children's transition to a new home and family. The move to a new environment and new relationships can be a difficult adjustment for any child. When the change includes new sights, sounds, and smells, coupled with an abrupt break from the past, a child can easily become overwhelmed. The use of transitional objects, particularly those that are sensually familiar to the child—photographs of both the former and the new home and people, for example—can be comforting.

Cultural differences in child-rearing, such as different methods of showing affection and different values, affect a child's transition. These contrasts may seem most relevant for older children; however, even infants notice changes in caregiving behaviors. American mothers and caregivers spend much less time holding their infants than caregivers in some other countries, for example. Necessary changes should be made gradually, with attention to the importance of maintaining ties to the child's cultural heritage.

One exception to the concept of gradual transition for children involves school attendance. School-aged children should be enrolled in school immediately rather than waiting for them to adjust to their new environment. The sooner the children are in a school setting, with appropriate grade-level placement and access to English-language programs for speakers of other languages, the more quickly and easily they will adjust.

Children's adjustment will also be easier if they live in an ethnically diverse neighborhood where they can meet other minority children and develop their own identities rather than trying to mold themselves to the dominant culture.

Reverse Prejudice

Internationally adopted children who have been successful at becoming Americanized frequently report difficulties fitting in with the people of their birth culture. A lack of command of the language and lack of knowledge of customs may be the issues that set them apart. An Asian American may feel not-quite-American based on his physical features and not-quite-Korean because he does not speak the language. He may, in fact, not carry or even know his Korean name.

The status of being adopted has a stronger social stigma in many developing countries than it does in this country. Social class issues are commonly involved in international adoption. Most of the children who are adopted internationally come from the lower socioeconomic groups. Because of their adoptive status, these children may be treated negatively by others from their birth country.

Ethnic prejudice based on coloring rather than race is also common in some countries. This prejudice exists in some Latin American countries, for example, and Latino American children need to be prepared to encounter bigotry from their own ethnic groups. This may be confusing to children who were brought up feeling very proud that they were Colombian or Brazilian, yet are treated with bigotry by other Latinos who may regard them as black.

Stereotyping

Both positive and negative stereotypes play a major role in how people view various racial and cultural minorities. These societal expectations pervade almost every facet of life and are difficult for children to overcome.

But these stereotypes are also subject to change. As an example, for many years Asians in America were regarded with fear and suspicion. When national attention turned to technology, an area in which Asians frequently excelled, they were suddenly admired for their intelligence, drive, and orderly behavior. Perhaps not surprisingly, Asian babies became highly desirable, "blue ribbon" solutions for American adopters who looked to international adoption as an answer to the shortage of Caucasian infants.

As much as the move to positive expectations would seem to benefit children, the opposite is true. Expectations, whether positive or negative, put too many burdens on children. Children who try to make their way in a vastly different land and culture are thrust into unrealistic expectations of behavior and performance.

Other problems also surface. As newly elevated minorities become chic, other racial minorities become more criticized. The result is an emotional backlash that stirs racial feelings and detracts from family efforts toward teaching acceptance.

What Parents Can Do

Parents need to start when their children are young to help them adjust to life as a racial minority in a different culture. Frequently this means that we must step outside our comfort zone, but it also gives us the opportunity to experience what our children experience every day by living in a dominant culture.

Helping Internationally Adopted Children Adjust

1. *Build diversity into your family life.* Do not limit your friendships to the groups that you and your child belong to. Live in a multiethnic neighborhood and celebrate the contributions of many peoples.
2. *Learn about your child's birth country and culture with him.* Provide him with many opportunities for learning, including language classes and culture camps so that he develops friendships with other children like himself. Retain his original name in some manner and encourage a homeland visit when he expresses an interest.
3. *Prepare your child for teasing.* Rehearse early and communicate that racism is a social, rather than a personal, issue. Create relationships with adults of your child's ethnic background who can say, "This is what we do when that happens."
4. *Present a positive or neutral image about adopting internationally.* Try to avoid focusing on the difficulties involved, such as poverty, street children, and corruption.
5. *Offer strong supports.* Let your child know that he can count on your unconditional love and support. Other critical supports include belief in God or a higher power and individual or family counseling for help with weighty issues.

18

OLDER CHILDREN

C hildren who are adopted at an older age have specialized needs that stem from their early life experiences and the loss of contact with important people in their lives. In the majority of older-child adoptions, the children have been a part of the foster care system (also known as interim care) or in an institutional living arrangement before permanent placement. In many cases these children's early life traumas were further compounded by the effects of institutional living, multiple moves, and additional broken relationships.

Foster care and some institutional living systems are intended to provide immediate, short-term care for children whose lives are in turmoil. Unfortunately, the likelihood of either kind of placement being used for extended, rather than limited, care, and their inherent lack of permanence place additional stresses on children.

Children who have lived with a number of different families through the foster care system—a common situation for American children—face the loss of important relationships and the challenge of forming new ones with every move. Children in institutional care—a common situation for international children—have greater stability but less individualized attention in what are often described as deprived environments.

Children in Care

Whereas orphans are not uncommon in international institutions, at present the number of true orphans in the United States foster care system is low. This situation is expected to change, however; by the year 2000 approximately 100,000 children are expected to be orphaned as a result of AIDS. Many of those children will enter the foster care system.

Most of the children who come into interim care in the United States are victims of poor parenting, that is, repeated abuse or ongoing neglect. Older children who enter care tend to come from a family situation that is dysfunctional, frequently as a result of parental mental illness, substance abuse, or youth.

Children who enter foster care in the United States are usually placed by court order rather than through voluntary parental relinquishment. Termination of parental rights occurs later primarily because reunification with the biological parents is not possible or not in the best interests of the child.

While the prevailing social-work theory in child welfare is family preservation, the number one priority is the safety of the children. During recent years, the foster care system in the United States has more than doubled in size, with the majority of children being placed in family foster care rather than institutional care.

Internationally, voluntary placement of older children is more common than it is in the United States. Children may be placed in an international orphanage because of catastrophic hardships or the stigma of raising children out of wedlock.

Regardless of the reason for placement, all of these children suffer from extreme turmoil. Permanent placement is often difficult to find. Prospective adoptive parents are frequently afraid of the baggage that the children may bring—lack of stability and an inability to form emotional attachments, for example.

Establishing Stability for Children

Three important factors contribute to the well-being of institutionalized children, regardless of whether the children find permanent placement or remain in care:

1. *Permanence and stability is paramount.* The children need to feel safe and secure, especially that they are protected from the abuses (or abusers) that brought them into care.

2. *Split loyalties must not be created.* The presence of kind and generous caregivers is important, but caregivers must not try to take the place of the children's birthparents. The children need to be accepted and loved for who they are.

   For adoptive parents, this takes a lot of wisdom. There are strong similarities to raising children of divorced parents. Children need to know that they can feel comfortable loving both parents, or both sets of parents.

3. *The children must feel unconditional love.* This means love that the children never have to earn; it must be unconditional whether or not the children ever accept the guidance and positive influences that are provided.

   The job of adoptive parents is to learn who the children are, then cultivate those unique personalities rather than imposing parental wishes. We need to say that we can accept and love these children exactly the way they are, not when their offensive behaviors are brought into line.

Children's Frustrations

Older children in care frequently have a history of multiple moves and broken relationships. With each new placement, the children are expected to change and adjust to new situations and new expectations. They must adjust to the family eating breakfast together or the way the family hammers out disagreements. They must learn what happens when rules are broken; in fact, that may be the way they learn what the rules are.

Eventually some children who are repeatedly placed in these situations give up trying to adapt and try to take control back themselves. They may stop trusting. For them love becomes abstract, a theoretical concept that never really fits them.

Another source of frustration to children who have experienced multiple placements is that they are frequently expected to forget their past and past relationships. In many cases, this denial of the children's past relationships is not explicitly communicated, but rather implicitly conveyed when the topic of the children's past is never brought up.

Adoptive parents must take care to have realistic expectations about their children. Adoption for older children is a step in their life, not the beginning of a new life. As adoptive parents we cannot sever our children from their past based on our expectations of a perfect family. Our children have birth relatives, past foster families, and friends, all of whom shared their lives. Despite the negative or positive influences that these relationships provided, we need to find value in them so that our children find value in themselves.

Many mental health specialists advise parents that they should not look for quick changes in their children's behaviors. A common rule of thumb is that parents should expect the same number of years to pass for a child to become unadjusted to past influences as the child's age when he entered the home. If you adopt a ten year old, for example, expect it to take approximately ten years to balance past influences.

Family Preparation

In order to help older children make a successful adjustment to permanent placement, adoptive families need preparation. They need to understand what to expect from their children, including an understanding of the children's history of broken relationships and the overwhelming effects that this would have on anyone's life.

Family preparation also involves an understanding of the family's role if a disruption should occur. Adoptive parents need to accept that in this case they must do whatever it takes to help the children ease out of the family.

Aids to Adjustment to Permanent Placement

1. *Avoid overenthusiasm.* "We are your forever family" makes a promise to the child that the family may not be able to keep. Using less loaded words, such as "We are happy that you're here. We want you to feel a part of our family," opens your heart to the child yet keeps expectations in perspective.
2. *Make use of post-placement family counseling from the outset.* Preplanned counseling allows an opportunity for family members to talk in a nonthreatening environment rather than waiting until a crisis occurs. The children can also benefit from observing an active approach to problem solving.
3. *Maintain sibling bonds.* Even if siblings cannot be placed together, continued opportunity for them to interact is crucial. Often siblings are the only form of connectedness that children have. They frequently

have a shared history that includes older children taking on parental roles for the younger children. (Adult adopted persons who have lost sibling contact often mourn that loss more than the loss of contact with their birthparents.)

4. *List the rules to the children.* A "here's what we do here" approach lets children know what the rules and consequences are before they find out by breaking the rules. It also shares the burden of communication with the parents by illuminating the idea that children cannot possibly know the limits of behavior without communication.

   Consequences need to be carefully thought out to avoid extremes of leniency or severity. They need to be applied consistently, especially for children who have grown up in institutions or who have lived with many different families. Depending on the ages of the children, it might be beneficial for parents to find out what the children's rules had been and what type of discipline was imposed for breaking those rules.

5. *Allow the children an opportunity to bring some of their customs or choices to the new family.* Letting them choose how to spend a family holiday, for example, immediately empowers them within the family and validates their past experiences.

6. *Make all transitions, even termination, gradual.* If termination occurs, the children should understand that it was the placement that was wrong, not the children or even the families.

19

OPENNESS

M any adoption advocates believe that open adoption relationships work well for children. An ongoing relationship with significant members of their own kinship system, they believe, gives children a better understanding of who they are while they are growing up. As the children of open adoptions have grown to adolescence, adoption professionals are learning that successful open adoptions are in evidence for children of all ages across the United States and Canada.

Open adoptions are also occurring across a broad range of adoption arrangements—infant adoptions in the United States, transracial adoptions, international adoptions, confidential adoptions that have become open, even public agency adoptions in which birthparents' rights have been terminated.

In the latter adoption situation, ways have been created for children to feel safe. Beyond safety, an additional area of concern for these children is to have linkage rather than a distinct cutoff from the birth family. In many cases, because of the importance of maintaining connectedness with siblings, open adoption is especially helpful for children with special needs.

Naming System

One of the more emotional obstacles in open adoption is the question of naming. By what name should each person in the extended relationship be called? When, for instance, does the birthmother stop being the mother and begin being just Susan? By what name is the birthmother's mother to be called? And, heaven forbid, how does the child explain who all these people are?

The difficulty with language is that it is so emotionally charged. As adoptive parents we struggle to use terminology that clarifies the roles of key people in our children's lives yet does not diminish our own roles at the same time.

With all adoptions, the emotional transfer of the child from birthparents to adoptive parents is a process rather than a single event for both the parents and the child. In infant adoptions, both birth and adoptive parents have time to adjust to their new roles; however, there may be an overlapping time of transition in which both birth and adoptive mothers are moms and both call the child "my baby." Eventually the transition is completed, and the task of assigning names with roles falls into place quite readily.

By the time the child is a toddler the birthparents often have become Chet and Susan. Birth grandparents, as well as others in the extended birth families, can be called by their birth relationships to the child (Grandma Melba) or their relationships to the birthparents (Susan's mother, Melba), whichever seems most comfortable. Birthparents are commonly called by their first names. They should not be called Aunt Susan and Uncle Chet, since that is an untruth and would need to be undone. An exception is when the birthmother or birthfather is the actual sister or brother of one of the adoptive parents. In this case the birthparents would be called Uncle Chet and Aunt Susan based on their new relationship to the child.

In older-child adoptions, the children have their own names established for each relative. This should, of course, be honored. The names of birthparents can be modified to

Mommy Susan and Daddy Chet, for example, similar to the naming systems that are used in stepparent households.

Children in open relationships will also be faced with answering the question, "How many brothers and sisters do you have?" If the extended birth families include the children of the birthparents, adopted children may wish to consider these children as siblings. This is another situation that is similar to extended stepfamily relationships in which children may have full siblings, half-siblings, and stepsiblings.

Successful Relationships

In a somewhat typical open adoption, birthparents are treated as close family members. Generally the role does not include co-parenting duties but does include the exchange of full identifying information, visitation (frequently in the child's home), and the gradual, time-appropriate disclosure of the birthparents' relationship to the child. In some open adoption relationships, children spend time at the homes of birthparents or birth grandparents, including holiday or vacation time visitations.

For an open relationship to be successful, you must feel comfortable, even happy, about the presence of your child's extended family. Otherwise your child will not feel happy. Your job as a parent, however, is not to see that the birthparents' needs are met but that your child's needs are met.

Adaptations

It is not uncommon that during the course of your ongoing relationship with the birthparents (either as a unit or as individuals), the intensity of the relationship may change. No human relationship is static, and your child's relationship with his birthparents is no exception. In fact, an adoption that was very open may change to resemble a semi-open adoption if the birthparents become inaccessible for any number of reasons and continued contact is limited to the exchange of information.

As the birthparents age, marry, give birth to other children, or relocate, their relationship with your child will vary. Weekly visits may change to monthly phone calls. Birthparents may even move into and out of your child's life. This is as normal a course of events as the changing relationship between your child and other relatives with whom he has an ongoing relationship. A favorite aunt may take a job overseas; grandparents may retire and move away.

Rather than mourn change, children should be helped to understand the normalcy of this process—that everyone, even the children themselves, gets busy with life. Our children's relationships with their birthparents should be similar to their relationships with other family members, neither stronger nor more influential. When grandparents are relocating, for example, we are likely to explain to our children, "We'll miss Grandpa and Grandma. They are moving because they want to live where it's warm. They are pretty busy with their lives," rather than "How dare they move away after building a relationship with you."

Over the course of years in an open adoption relationship, children may see their birthparents demonstrating a wide range of behaviors. They may see their birthparents not achieving goals or having to place other children, to name a few. (Or, for that matter, they may see the birthparents achieving stability while their adoptive parents divorce.)

Your child cannot control any of these decisions and actions. What you can do as a family is to continue to love the birthparents and continue to welcome them. Parents can say to their children, "We've done everything we can as a family. Our door will always be open to Daddy Chet. We will always care about him." Children do quite well with that approach rather than when their parents try to protect them from disappointment.

Mental health professionals who work with families involved in open adoption suggest that, like family members, birthparents and their extended family members who behave in a manner that is inappropriate to the well-being of your child be treated accordingly. Your parental duty is to step in and alter the situation, including severing ties with the individual if appropriate.

Children involved in open adoptions do as well as the adults do about it. The goal, as in all adoption situations, is to have an attitude that the situation is no better nor worse than any other family situation.

Play Groups

Adoption specialists are finding that children of open adoption need the same sorts of play groups as other groups of adopted children. Children who are growing up in open adoption are at present a minority among adopted people. Knowing other children in open adoption helps them establish normalcy. Like children adopted transracially, children growing up in open adoption need to know others like themselves.

Parents can create opportunities for interaction through a variety of methods, including pen pals, field trips, or picnics with other children growing up in open adoption.

Prejudice

An interesting social phenomenon has been occurring for some children who are growing up in open adoption. Rather than prejudice from non-adopted people, who never seem to understand open adoption anyway, the children of open adoption are experiencing a backlash from families whose children are growing up in confidential adoptions.

Families in open adoptions choose not to deal with secrets. Their relationships with their children's extended birth families are on the table. All this openness tends to raise issues for children with whom there is secrecy about adoption, especially when that secrecy is, for the most part, a matter of choice by the adoptive parents.

This backlash is another illustration of the importance of friendships with other children who are growing up in open adoption.

20

~~~~~~

CONFIDENTIALITY

Once the standard in American adoptions, confidential adoptions have become one of a number of choices of adoption styles. Today most confidential adoptions are so by choice rather than by custom.

A modern adoption may be confidential due to: (1) the adoptive parents' personal beliefs in the value of confidentiality in adoption, (2) a previous confidential adoption of another child in the family and the parents' desire for subsequent adoptions to be similar, (3) uncontrollable circumstances, such as a lack of background information, (4) the wishes of the birthparent(s), or (5) the perceived best interests of the child to not have contact with birth relatives.

Confidentiality continues to be somewhat standard in international adoptions. It is not uncommon in same-race, transracial, or older-child adoptions within the United States and Canada. It should be noted, however, that as the children age and families face issues related to the children's identity formation, many adoptions that were formerly confidential become more open as families seek information about their children's background or establish relationships with the children's birth relatives.

Available Information

In truth, very few modern adoptions, especially placements within the United States, are completely confidential; most adoptions involve some exchange of information between birth and adoptive parents. The exchange may be made without identifying information being passed, and the birth and adoptive parents may never meet. The majority of international placements continue to be more confidential than adoptions in this country.

In adoptions within the United States and Canada that are considered confidential, birthparents frequently receive a written description and possibly a photograph of the prospective adopters and may, in fact, have the opportunity to choose from a list of prospective adopters provided by the adoption professional.

Adoptive families generally receive written social and medical background information about the birthparents and, commonly, the reasons for adoptive placement. If more information is needed, for a medical emergency, for example, adoptive parents may be able to gain access to additional genetic or health information via their adoption professional while continuing to maintain confidentiality.

Children placed for adoption frequently are given letters or mementos as keepsakes from their birthparents, often with an invitation for the children to establish contact when they reach adulthood, if they desire.

Effects on Children
With the rise in openness in adoption, society has begun to expect that adoptive parents and adopted children have a degree of knowledge about the children's birthparents or birth histories. When such information is not available, children in confidential adoptions may feel slighted by not having the information that other adopted children have about their backgrounds. These children, who were once in the majority of adopted persons, may regret that they, too, do not have access to information about themselves or an opportunity to interact with their birth relatives.

Much has been said about an adopted child's need for the self-identity that comes from knowledge about her background and genetic heritage. If your child was adopted through a confidential adoption, you can still help her to use the knowledge that she does have to form a more complete image of herself. This is similar to the cultural openness approach used in international adoptions, in which adopted persons and their families discover historical and cultural information about the children's backgrounds rather than having face-to-face encounters with birth relatives. You may, for example, know which part of the country your child was born in and visit the locale to help her gain a greater understanding of the customs and traditions of the people of that area.

Her personal story could include comforting suppositions based on the information that is available, such as "We don't know a whole lot about your birthparents, but we do know that they were both young and in school when you were born. I'll bet that they knew that it was important for them to go to school and that they couldn't take care of a baby at that time in their lives. It must have been very hard for them to have made the decision to make an adoption plan for you. They must have loved you very much."

You can also help your child make her life book based on available information: pictures of the hospital where she was born, photos of interesting architecture of the area, and descriptions of the ways in which many of the people in that area make their livelihood, for example. Copies of newspaper headlines from the time of her birth or the words to popular songs that her birthparents might have listened to can help her formulate a mental picture of her background. (See Key 10 for information on personal stories and life books for your child.)

Access to play groups or support groups with other children of confidential adoption may prove helpful.

Mental health professionals experienced in adoption issues believe in the importance of truthful and complete disclosure of background information to children whenever that information is available. Of course, care needs to be taken to discuss adoption issues in ways that are appropriate to the child's level of understanding, and, if a difficult background is a part of the child's history, parents should be sensitive when disclosing such information.

Opening Communication

Over the course of time, some adoptions that began as confidential may change to semi-open or open adoptions. Adoptive or birth parents may change their views about the advisability of openness and agree to some degree of contact. The advantages of greater access to medical or genetic information may become important to the health or well-being of the children. Or the adopted individuals themselves may desire more information or contact when they approach adulthood.

As a result of changes in laws about access to records, many adoptions that begin as confidential—and were expected to remain so—may eventually become open when adopted children reach adulthood. Adopted persons and birthparents are gaining greater access to records and finding ways in which confidentiality can be breached.

Your Child's Desire for Information

Not all adopted people want access to more information about their birth history. Of those who do search for more, the majority are content with uncovering information or meeting their birth relatives. Although they may express curiosity about their genetic relationships, most do not wish to initiate a relationship with their birth relatives.

If the idea of your child desiring more information about her background is upsetting to you, you may be subconsciously conveying your fears to your child. Adult adopted persons frequently report that these fears on the part of their parents do not result in the abandonment of the search. Rather the result is a secret search or postponement of the search until after the death of the adoptive parents.

Openly confronting your fears or challenging their validity is often helpful. Try speaking with members of an adoption support group or reading one of the many revealing books about adoptive searches and meetings. You may be surprised to learn of the experiences of other worried parents who faced their fears and helped their children conduct a search. These parents frequently relate a deepened relationship with their children, rather than the weakened ties that they had feared. Assisting your child with a search may be a meaningful and liberating experience for both you and your child.

Part Four

~~~~~~

SPECIAL RISK ISSUES

I
f you are raising a child with special adoption needs, you
know that parenting is not about kids making adults feel
good. It is about parents helping kids feel good. For parents of special-needs children, including the many who find
permanent placement as older children, parenting is both
developmental and therapeutic.

Among the special issues that children may bring to adoptive placement are attachment disorders, attention deficit disorders, substance exposure, sexual abuse, and difficult background information.

These issues are risk factors that may interfere with a
child's successful adjustment. The needs may have been
apparent before placement—they may even have been the
reasons that brought the child to adoptive placement. Or
they may not have appeared until after placement.

Regardless of the exact circumstances, special-needs
children are the products of extreme emotional upheaval.
You can be assured that if your child's scars are not on the
outside, they are on the inside.

Chronic Difficult Behaviors

Many children with special adoption issues exhibit difficult behaviors. Parents who adopt older children expect that
their children will have certain emotional problems stemming
from multiple placements and a history of broken relationships. Parents who adopt children in infancy cannot be guar-
anteed that their children will be spared serious behavior

problems. Although parents may or may not have been aware of the potential for difficult behaviors before placement, coping with the behaviors and the stresses that they put on the family unit can be especially trying.

Adoption specialists recognize that many adoptive parents are willing to tackle the challenge of parenting children with difficult behaviors when they know exactly what to expect. Living with a child with chronic serious behavior problems requires more than just preparation, however. Parents need to develop support systems for their children and themselves to help the family through the inevitable crises. Parents also need to be willing to postpone even simple gratifications of parenting, content in the knowledge that without the family bonds, the affected child would probably be suffering even more intensely.

Frequently caregivers misinterpret the signals of special-needs children because of the children's skills in survival behaviors. Parents tend to view the behaviors as being either manipulative or attention-seeking. These behaviors, which can be extremely taxing, put additional stress on families and relationships. Even after professional intervention, these behaviors may jeopardize the children's successful adoptive placement.

Childhood Depression

Many of the behaviors that had previously been associated with older-child adoption are now being reassessed. These behaviors—which often surface as anger, hostility, lack of concentration, lack of motivation, even lack of intelligence—are being reexamined as side effects of childhood depression. They may be child-expressed attempts to take back control of the environment. At any rate, they are the external demonstrations of the emotional baggage that children carry. Like a bad back that causes foot problems due to an uneven stance, children's emotional baggage may in turn cause other problems.

Childhood depression is largely due to the emotional upheaval that has brought children into care in the first place. Add to this the shortcomings of institutionalization and the abrupt loss of significant people in their life whom they trusted and loved and who cared for them, no matter how inadequately.

As adoptive parents, we tend to think our expectations are reasonable. "All I ask is that he turn in his homework assignments," we protest. While we are focusing on math assignments, our children may be preoccupied with bigger issues, such as grieving the loss of past relationships. Sadly, we cannot always know what our children feel. Often the children are doing the best they can to survive.

21

~~~~~~

ATTACHMENT DISORDERS

M any special-needs children exhibit attachment difficulties. These difficulties can be attributed to the family situation that brought the children to adoptive placement or to the effects of multiple caregivers—and multiple broken attachments—through the interim care system. They may also be the consequences of environments that lack proper stimulation, such as international orphanages, especially if the institutions did not provide much individual attention.

Lack of attaching is a defense mechanism for children. It shields them from the disappointment of broken promises. Past abuses may make children feel that they are not deserving of love and attention, and flashbacks to that abuse may cause them to pull away. Children really do want to be close but, in many cases, their prior experiences have taught them that closeness hurts.

Regardless of the reasons, attachment disorders are common in special-needs and older-child adoptions. It should be noted, however, that while attachment disorders exist, the frequency of actual unattached children is very small. The task for caregivers is to undo the effects of the children's past relationships and work to build their own positive attachments.

Behaviors

A child with an attachment disorder may be extremely disruptive and abusive. Commonly, aggression and obnoxious behavior are taken out on the mother and may result in maternal depression, which in turn may cause problems in the extended family or the marriage. Often the family is blamed for the problem: "If only you had more love and parenting skills," they are told.

The behaviors of children with attachment difficulties are often the result of the defense mechanisms that they have developed. Children with attachment difficulties exhibit fairly typical behaviors. These include:

• Physical or emotional distance from adults. These children do not look to adults or their parents for stimulation or comfort; they may avoid eye contact with adults.

• Excessive dependence or independence. The children are frequently either overly anxious or socially isolated. These behaviors may be predictable or they may be erratic in a push-pull manner with parents.

• Lack of awareness of either self or environment. Some children are so tuned into themselves that they are oblivious of their environment; others are the reverse.

• Controlling behaviors. The children are hostile and seem to view every situation as a win-lose battle.

• Lack of a fear of consequences. These are the children whom parents label as "without conscience." Attempts to threaten or manipulate such children fall short. The children tend to lack attachment to both people and physical possessions.

• Indiscriminate shows of affection. These children are labeled *ambivalently attached*. They are frequently described as charming to other adults and openly hostile to their parents.

- Learning difficulties. Children with attachment disorders may exhibit learning difficulties merely because of their past histories—a series of disappointments, difficulty in forming new relationships, or fear that their abuser may return. Concentrating on school assignments may be the least of their worries.

Overall, parents seem to have the most difficulty with children who are ambivalently attached, those who at one moment are clinging to their caregivers and the next moment assaulting them. This love-hate behavior is a result of the opposite feelings of rejection or betrayal paired with a craving for love and affection.

Treatments

Regardless of the children's behaviors, the job of parents is to meet the children's needs. Children need positive attention, but they need to learn new ways to achieve that positive attention. Parents need to be sensitive to their children's signals as well as initiate a variety of interactions with the children.

The problem with attachment disorders is that there really is not one good, specific treatment. Progress is usually slow and frequently requires professional assistance. This is one of those situations in which love does not cure everything. Major family problems can occur if an attachment disorder is not addressed.

Therapies that have been successful for attachment disorders have a number of common factors. These include focused attention, physical touch, and decoding of children's behaviors.

Focused attention is a specific period of time dedicated to one-on-one interaction between parent and child. The time is preselected, and the child, rather than his misbehavior, is the center of attention.

Physical touch is very important in all human relationships and is especially critical in helping children build attachments. Many special-needs children have been touch deprived. Others just need to benefit from close interaction with another caring person.

The third component of a successful plan in dealing with attachment disorders lies in correctly interpreting the child's behaviors. The anger that many special-needs children seem to exhibit, for example, is actually fear.

Therapists recommend that parents of special-needs children keep journals of their children's progress. These journals can show behavior patterns—which behaviors are chronic or rhythmic, for example—and where progress in behavior changes appears.

Building Positive Attachments

In addition to strategies that involve focused attention, physical touch, and accurate decoding of children's behaviors, exposure to appropriate behaviors is critically important for special-needs children. Children who do not know how to handle anger or closeness, for example, need to observe caregivers who exhibit appropriate reactions to those feelings and situations.

Factors for Building Positive Attachments

1. *Time.* Children benefit from learning that relationships with significant people can be changed and improved over a course of time. They can see that relationships are built gradually, that they can be improved through direct efforts, and that they can be developed into dependable situations that provide ongoing strength and enjoyment.

2. *New, repeated experiences with others.* Opportunities for positive relationships with others illustrate that interactions can be enjoyable and that they can be shared with a variety of other people, such as friends at school.

3 *A strong emotional experience.* A major trauma or a significant emotional experience can bring about dramatic change in children's attachments. A catastrophic natural occurrence—a hurricane, for example—can illustrate to an unattached child that people who know and care about each other find ways of pulling together to deal with a significant life experience, that families gain strength rather than disintegrate through adversity.

22

ΛΛΛΛΛΛΛΛΛΛΛΛΛΛΛΛΛΛΛΛΛΛΛΛΛΛΛΛΛΛΛΛΛΛΛΛΛΛΛΛΛΛΛΛΛΛΛΛΛΛΛΛΛΛΛΛΛΛ

ATTENTION DEFICIT DISORDER

I mpulsive, impatient, distractable children often stand out behaviorally from their adoptive parents. These are generally the behaviors attributed to children with Attention Deficit Disorder, or ADD.

Attention deficit disorder is a common chronic disorder of childhood that affects approximately five percent of the school-age population. Attention deficit disorder is presumed to be primarily a physiological dysfunction associated with environmental and social influences. The underlying cause of ADD is not always clearly differentiated from that of other childhood disorders.

Some attention deficit specialists suggest that a greater number of adopted than non-adopted children exhibit symptoms of ADD. Although its exact cause is unknown, some of the risk factors that appear to be linked to the disorder are fairly common in adopted children. These links are related to genetics, prenatal conditions, and early life experiences.

Conversely, some non-adopted children with undiagnosed ADD may not stand out behaviorally from their parents and, thus, are not identified as having the condition. A large number of undiagnosed children with ADD symptoms would alter the statistics that presently point to a higher rate of ADD in adopted children.

There appears to be a genetic link in ADD, particularly between fathers and sons. In addition, parents with crisis pregnancies or who are unable to parent their children may be prone to the impulsive, less-than-cautious behaviors typical of ADD. In utero conditions may also be contributors—poor prenatal care or alcohol or tobacco use, for example—and may increase children's risk for ADD. A third risk factor often associated with adopted children is insecurity in early life experiences. Many of the behaviors associated with disruptions and stresses in young children can cause a number of problems, such as ADD, later in life.

Because children with ADD often demonstrate many of the same behaviors as children with learning disabilities (LD), ADD is commonly linked to learning disabilities. Despite the apparent similarities, the two terms are not synonymous or causal. Learning disabilities cannot cause ADD and ADD cannot cause learning disabilities. Although it is true that some children can have both ADD and LD, most children with ADD do not have LD and most children with LD do not have ADD. A child with undiagnosed ADD will have trouble in school; once the condition is properly diagnosed and treated, the child's performance at school should improve.

Diagnosis

One of the difficulties in the diagnosis of ADD is the difference between physical and psychological behaviors, that is, the difference between whether the child has control or does not have control of his actions.

Researchers compiled a list of fourteen possible symptoms of ADD in *The Diagnostic and Statistical Manual of Mental Disorders—Revised of the American Psychiatric Association* (1987). The criteria used to diagnose ADD state that a child must have at least eight of the fourteen symptoms. The symptoms must appear before the age of seven and must last for at least six months.

Indicators of Attention Deficit Disorder
The child:

- fidgets,
- has difficulty remaining seated when instructed,
- is easily distracted,
- is impatient,
- blurts out responses,
- has difficulty completing instructions,
- lacks concentration or focus,
- shifts from one uncompleted activity to another,
- is noisy,
- talks excessively,
- intrudes or interrupts,
- does not listen,
- loses necessary items,
- is physically impulsive.

Because of the recent "popularity" of ADD, parents should guard against a too-hasty diagnosis. The best way to determine if your child has ADD is to have her evaluated by a multidisciplinary team of medical, psychological, educational, and social work professionals.

Treatment Options
The most effective treatment for ADD has been a combination of medical and psychological therapy. The medications currently used to treat ADD are safe and effective. The vast majority of children and young adults who have been properly diagnosed show improvement when they are treated with psychostimulant medication, when appropriate, in conjunction with behavior management techniques, intervention in the school, and counseling.

Medication

Parents often wonder about the advisability of medical intervention and, if it is recommended, when the time is appropriate to begin treatment. One important consideration must be the physical safety and well-being of the child and family. If the child is running uncontrolled into the street, medication may be appropriate for her safety. Likewise, if the child has faced expulsion from a string of day cares, interrupting the failure experience may be an important issue.

Medication does not always work in predictable patterns, but when it works, it does wonders. The success creates a spiral effect that builds on the child's increased sense of self-esteem.

Behavioral techniques

Parent education and training is critical in the effectiveness of treating children with ADD. Children who are impulsive and easily distractable will not benefit from one-hour sessions with an ADD specialist. What benefits them is a structured, consistent environment that enables them to learn good self-control.

Parents who learn successful techniques for helping their children can provide the environment and teach the coping skills that will help the children succeed. Approaches based on reinforcement for appropriate behavior and consequences for inappropriate behavior have been very effective.

Successful acceptance of the children's condition also includes the "guardian angel" strategy, in which parents help the children get in control rather than continuously battling the children's negative behaviors. This includes techniques such as teaching the children how to handle stressful situations through sensory relaxation or using nonverbal signals to prompt the children to stop and think through their actions.

Coping Mechanisms for Parents

Children who exhibit the characteristics of ADD can be very frustrating. Many of their behaviors are annoying and can seem to stem from laziness or obstinacy. Parents who have been successful at controlling many facets of their lives often do not know where to turn when their intelligence, intuition, and education fall short in helping them change their children's undesirable behaviors. First-time parents wonder if the children's behaviors are "normal" and, if so, how much more they can tolerate. The possibility of a physical disorder is often not suggested until the children's behaviors become unsafe or behavioral problems surface in the school setting.

A diagnosis of ADD presents parents with the additional burden that their children actually have a disorder, and that their behaviors are not something that will improve with age or a little more discipline.

One of the most effective ways for parents to deal with children's attention deficit disorder is to start by accepting that the children have the condition. This means facing the difference between their expectations for the children (and for the parenting experience) and the reality of the situation.

Once parents get over their initial disappointment and anger and move on to acceptance, they are ready to make the best of the situation and see things begin to change.

23

∿∿

SUBSTANCE EXPOSURE

Children can be exposed to parental substance abuse in a variety of ways. They may be exposed in utero to substances used by their parents, particularly their mothers. They may inherit a genetic tendency to an addiction, such as alcoholism. They may also suffer exposure by living in a home environment where the abuse of alcohol, tobacco, legal medications, and/or illegal drugs occurs. Heavy caffeine consumption is also suspected to adversely affect children in utero.

The effects of substance exposure on children can be physical or behavioral. Children who were exposed in utero may be born with physical birth defects or mental retardation. Many children have nerve damage that affects their entire system and causes such effects as eating, sleeping, or learning disorders.

While these substances have certain identifiable effects or clusters of effects, individual children's reactions to a particular substance can vary a great deal. When there is a parental history of drug abuse, a child can have all, some, or none of the effects. Sometimes damage is apparent right away; other times it does not appear until adulthood, when reproductive problems appear.

Identifying Exposure

Substance exposure can best be identified at birth. Three methods have been proven to be most effective: an umbilical cord blood test, infant hair analysis, and the infant's first bowel movement. Other methods—urine tests and birth-mother history, for example—tend to miss a significant number of children who have been exposed to substances.

Beyond birth, substance exposure is hard to determine. Also, once a child has spent any amount of time in a deprived home environment or in foster care, it is difficult to decide what causes abnormal behaviors.

Some adoption experts believe that a large population of substance-exposed children is not being identified. Most of the mothers who are screened for substance exposure before delivery are lower-socioeconomic-class or minority women. Middle- and upper-class white mothers are not routinely tested and their children are not routinely evaluated. Also, some birthmothers who wish to make an adoption plan may hide information about substance abuse because they want their children to have the best possible opportunities.

Symptoms

The effects of substance exposure vary with the nature of the substance, the manner in which the child is exposed, the frequency and duration of use, and the individual child's degree of resiliency.

Heavy alcohol consumption in pregnant women can cause birth abnormalities in children. A condition known as fetal alcohol syndrome, or FAS, is immediately recognizable at birth since it results in physical abnormalities. Babies born with FAS tend to be shorter and lighter in weight. They also tend to have abnormal features of the face and head. Behavioral abnormalities result from central nervous system damage and may include clumsiness, body rock, inability to think abstractly, math difficulties, short- and long-term memory problems, poor attention span, hyperactivity, extreme nervousness, and weak cause-and-effect thinking skills. Mental retardation is common.

A similar but less severe condition, fetal alcohol effect, does not cause the physical abnormalities of FAS, but the behavioral characteristics are the same.

The effects of cocaine and heroin tend to be similar to each other. Common outcomes for pregnant women who use these substances include miscarriages and early delivery. Children who have been exposed to cocaine and heroin tend to suffer from low birth weight, eating disorders, sleeping disorders, inability to concentrate, and eye problems. Urogenital abnormalities may also appear, primarily with cocaine exposure. In addition, cocaine causes a small lesion in the brain, which produces dramatic mood swings.

One of the most apparent symptoms of in utero substance exposure in children is hypersensitivity—to foods, to noises, to distractions. This hypersensitivity disrupts children's normal growth and development. It obstructs their ability to learn and interferes with their ability to be comforted.

Adaptations

Regardless of the actual causes of physical or behavioral abnormalities, little can be done to reverse the effects. Background knowledge is helpful in alerting parents to possible difficulties, but for the most part, even if the information is known, the effects cannot be fixed. Some adaptations are possible—teaching children how to learn in different ways, for example—but there is really no way these outcomes can be changed with medicine, therapy, or other interventions. Parents need to stop searching for a cause because they cannot go back and undo the damage. To be most effective, parents need to come to terms with their children's needs and use that knowledge to teach their children how to live and compensate.

There are effective ways to respond to children who are hypersensitive, for example. These include providing children with:

- safety and security,
- structured environments,
- help in school,
- therapeutic holding,
- limitation or removal of distractions,
- prevention of overstimulation,
- a consistent yet flexible schedule,
- methods of care and comforting that work with infants,
- lowered expectations.

Another technique is for parents to compensate rather than insist. For example, parents can use a nutritional supplement while trying to work on feeding problems so the child receives adequate nutrition while his parents are trying to work on long-term solutions. A child with sleeping disorders can be allowed to play in his room at night provided he is safe and distractions are kept to a minimum.

Parents can expect that improvement will come and go and that undesirable behaviors will come back during periods of high stress. It is almost as though the exterior stresses of the world work on the interior stresses of the children. When regression does occur, parents need to return to the things that provide comfort for the children, such as warm, soft foods. Some children will outgrow some of the problems and get better. Others will not.

Love obviously isn't enough, but love is where it starts. Our children need to know that they have our unconditional love and that we think they are special. Regardless of their difficulties, however, children can learn and should be expected to learn socially appropriate ways to express their frustrations.

Helping Children Understand

Children can be very angry and frustrated about the shortcomings that they suffer as a result of the actions of adults that the children were powerless to prevent. Just as parents need to come to grips with the reality of the situation, children need to be helped with acceptance. Like adoption, like eye and skin color, some things just happen to people.

Most children can understand the concept of addiction. They can also be helped to learn about and value their birthparents' good genetic qualities.

Creating life books and meeting other children who share some of the same experiences and feelings can be enormously helpful to children who have experienced substance exposure.

24

SEXUAL ABUSE

E stimates vary as to exact numbers, but many adoption professionals believe that the vast majority of children who become eligible for adoption through the foster care system have a history of sexual abuse. For parents of children who have been sexually abused, the task is to determine how they can help their children in their healing process and how they can intervene to help their children not start their own cycle of abusive behavior.

Sexual trauma is not something that children forget or get over. It does not go away if you ignore it, and it cannot be resolved with a handful of therapy sessions. It is usually an issue that children will need to return to as they reach new developmental stages and issues in their lives. Even after intensive therapeutic work, children often need to process this again at later stages in life.

The actions of children who have been sexually abused often make grownups uncomfortable. Most adoptive parents did not plan on having to deal with the effects of sexual abuse when they decided to adopt. They react by wanting to find the one magic action that will fix things for their children. Unfortunately, this is not available. What parents can do is be with their children during the healing process and provide resources and support systems. The "fix-it" people who must do the work of healing are the children themselves.

Indicators of Abuse

Children who have been sexually abused may act out in several ways, including repeating what they have been taught by their abusers.

Signs of Sexual Abuse

Sexual behaviors that are not age appropriate:

- knowledge of body parts or sexual acts that are not appropriate for the child's age
- excessive or public masturbation
- acts of sexual aggression toward siblings
- sexually suggestive actions toward adults

Other reactions:

- fear
- anger
- chronic helplessness

Some children will show and tell adults what happened to them. They may reenact the trauma by using dolls, another child, or the family pet.

Other children, especially those who were abused at a young age, may have no conscious memory of the abuse. At later developmental stages, however, sensory perceptions, such as certain smells or songs, may trigger reminders of the abuse.

Whether or not there are clear indicators of sexual abuse, the probability of a history of sexual abuse among children who are adopted at an older age is high. Parents who adopt school-age children should assume that abuse has occurred and prepare for it. Adopters of younger children, however, should not assume that abuse has not occurred.

Impact of Abuse

How children react to sexual abuse experiences and what the impact will be on them immediately and in the long term depend on a number of variables. These include the nature of the abuse; the relationship between the child and the abuser; the frequency, intensity, and duration of the abuse; and the manipulative methods used by the abuser to ensure the child's secrecy. Other factors influencing the severity of the trauma include the emotional strengths and supports available to the child before and after the abuse. Generally, the more traumatic the abuse and the weaker the supports, the stronger the effects.

Older children who have been sexually abused frequently report that the worst thing that happened to them was not the abuse but the loss of relationships that followed—the abandonment by the birthmother, the move into the foster care system, or the loss of contact with siblings, for example—and the implicit message that children are to be used and discarded as worthless.

Guilt and pleasure associated with the experience, and love and hatred for the perpetrator, especially when the abuser is a parent, are not uncommon feelings for children who have been abused. Parts of their sexual experience may have been pleasurable—receiving special attention, for example—while other parts may have been frightening or painful. If children experienced pleasure in association with an action that they label bad, they are likely to see themselves as being bad.

Statistically, a child who has been abused once is more likely to be abused again than a child who has never been abused. This appears to have a direct relationship to the poor or negative self-image that abused children are likely to have.

Helping Children
Even though most adoptive parents were not in a position to influence their children's support systems before abuse

occurred or to prevent it from happening, they can influence the support that is available to the children afterward.

Parents should accept what the children tell them without quibbling over the details of the story. Adults may be uncomfortable, even repulsed, by the details that children reveal. It is important that parents put aside these feelings to allow the children to speak openly and to not feel that they are either responsible or repulsive.

Children who have experienced sexual trauma need to have their feelings accepted as real and valid. They also need reassurance that inappropriate or hurtful things can look or feel good at the same time and that it is possible to love someone even after that person does hurtful things. Parents can tell their children that sometimes the difference between grown-up, or sexual, touching and good touch can be confusing and that they will help them learn about sharing good loving.

Many therapists who have experience dealing with sexual abuse stress the importance of eliminating judgmental terminology when speaking with children about abuse. They believe that it is of critical importance to remove the words *bad* and *wrong* from any association with the children's early sexual experiences so that the children do not label themselves bad by having been involved in those experiences.

Children who have been sexually abused do not know about healthy sexuality as a part of human development at every age. The extent of their understanding is about sex used as power, sex used in anger, sex used to hurt, and sex used as stimulation.

Parents can help by teaching their children that although sexuality is important for every person, the sexuality that is appropriate for children is different than what is appropriate for adults. Even young children can understand that some sexual actions are okay for grownups but not for children—Daddy patting Mommy on the derriere, for example. Preschool children can understand that learning about their bodies is a natural thing for four year olds to do, and that as they grow up they will learn more. Older children can learn about privacy, about physical and sexual maturity, and about sexuality as a part of love and affection between adults.

Professional therapeutic intervention is recommended for children who have been sexually abused. A children's mental health therapist who has experience in both sexual abuse and adoption issues can help children through the immediate situation and crises that may arise later on.

Family and group counseling is frequently more effective than traditional individual counseling for children who have experienced sexual abuse, particularly in dealing with the secrecy upon which sexual abuse often thrives. Children who abuse other children or pets need immediate and ongoing therapeutic intervention in order to break out of these destructive patterns.

Needs of Sexually Abused Children

1. *Acceptance.* Parents can help their children by conveying their sadness that the children were hurt but gratification that they can talk about it together. Children need to know that they are good and lovable and that their parents' love for them will not change even if terrible things happen to them.

   Access to support groups of other children who have been abused is a good way for children to begin healing and to lessen the feelings of isolation and alienation.

2. *Safety.* Children need to know that the actions of the adult were wrong, and that children have a right to

be protected, loved, and cared for by adults. They also need to feel safe from continued contact with the perpetrator.

3. *An understanding of sexuality as a part of human development.* Children can understand that grown-up sexual acts are not the job of a child. The job of a child is to learn about being a boy or girl, to make friends, and to be good in school. Grownups who give children the job of an adult (a sexual act, for example) are wrong and should have known better.

4. *Control of their environment.* Allowing children to make decisions and take control of certain situations is also helpful for those who have been sexually abused.

   An additional benefit of allowing children to have some control is that they develop a sense of responsibility for what happens. This allows children who have been abused to move from a feeling of being a victim to one of being a survivor.

5. *Consequences for their behavior.* Sometimes children will continue to act out inappropriately to rile adults and maintain things at a crisis level. A neutral response from adults, such as, "That is not appropriate behavior. It's not what we do in this family. This is the consequence of the behavior. I know you will figure out how to behave in the right way because you are smart and I will help you with it," and the follow-through, teach children that they cannot take control through inappropriate actions.

6. *Rituals and routines.* Children who have been sexually abused may be accustomed to erratic routines and rituals that are associated with their abuse. These can be replaced by family patterns that celebrate positive experiences. Working together as a

family unit, for example, is a situation in which each individual is important and belongs to the unit.

7. *Spirituality.* Children who have been hurt need to feel a sense of hope, that there is goodness in the universe. They need to feel that there is a connection between them, a higher power, and the universe and that they deserve to be a part of it.

25

DIFFICULT BACKGROUND INFORMATION

A history of violence, abuse, or abandonment by a birthparent is just one of several unpleasant situations that might be part of an adopted child's background. Other powerfully negative background information includes racism as a reason for adoptive placement, neglect, domestic violence between birthparents, handicaps, multiple births, mental illness, or conception issues, such as rape, incest, or attempted abortion.

Most adoption professionals believe that even difficult information like this needs to be shared with adopted persons at an appropriate time to help them construct realistic identities and positive self-concepts.

Parents cannot erase the hurts for children, but by supporting them and by being sensitive and truthful, they can be the families that the children need.

Building a Foundation

As hard as it may be for parents to share difficult information with their children, the children have the right to full disclosure of their genetic heritage and background. The timing and delivery of this information is of critical importance, however. The telling of sensitive birth-family information requires great care and delicacy, and attention to the developmental readiness of the child.

Parents can begin early to set the stage for this disclosure by fostering attitudes of tolerance and compassion. This goes beyond merely talking about acceptance. It means that parents' words and actions must demonstrate their belief in the worth of every human being.

Families can take advantage of media stories to discuss the stresses and circumstances that lead to troubled behaviors, for example. This helps children separate judgment of deed from evaluations of people. Parents also need to emphasize the detachment of the victim from the deed—that is, children whose parents commit unpleasant acts against them are not responsible for the actions of the adults.

Parents should convey that the birth of every baby is cause for celebration. Even if adults have concerns about the welfare of the child, every baby is inherently something to be valued, no matter how he was conceived, and every person has opportunities for growth and change.

Sharing Positive Information

When parents communicate positive or neutral information about birthparents to their children early on, they enable their children to balance the negative information about their biological parents when it is presented later. The knowledge of positive information about birthparents also helps children with their unspoken questions of "Am I going to be like my birthparents when I grow up?" Information about birthparents' strengths, talents, and interests can provide children with a foothold as they build their own character.

If specific information is unavailable, parents can use inferences. If your child has an outgoing personality, you can say, "I'll bet there's someone in your birth family who is friendly just like you are. That's a nice quality. It makes other people feel good."

Parents can tell young children factual information without disclosing all the details they would reveal to older children. They need to start the discussion early and to always be truthful, so the children know that they can depend upon their parents to give them the correct story. Another story or version should never be substituted. If your child eventually wants to conduct a search, you do not want to be in the position of having intentionally provided misinformation.

Developmental Readiness

Children's questions can be a good guide to their readiness to learn about their background. Parents have the best knowledge of their own children, and, with the help of education and the shared experiences of other parents, are the best decision makers about what is right for their children.

Although parents may be understandably reluctant to discuss unpleasant issues with their children, the truth is often less overwhelming to children than their fears or worries. Children soon learn that if their parents avoid a subject, that subject is considered taboo. The unspoken message is that the subject is something shameful and something for which the children had some responsibility.

Many experts believe that while parents do need to share information with their children, the disclosure of strongly, negative information is best postponed until middle childhood or late adolescence (depending on the individual child's emotional readiness), when children have a greater ability to be objective and realistic in shouldering the information. However, withholding information until then requires that parents be discreet about sharing with others information that the children have not yet learned.

In the meantime, parents can initiate discussions on not using power to hurt or intimidate, and on the importance of trying to understand the reasons behind people's behaviors. This does not excuse behaviors; it merely tries to understand them and offer hope for change.

A four year old whose conception was the result of rape could be told the available information about his birthmother and that not much information is available about his birthfather. When he is eight, he can be told that his birthmother did not have a good relationship with his birthfather, that his birthmother was not ready at that time to be a parent, and that she wanted the child to be raised by both a mother and father who cared about him. For an older child or young adult, there should be some disclosure once the child's own sense of worth is intact.

If the child is of mixed racial heritage, parents need to take care not to imply that the birthfather, by his violent act, is representative of his entire racial group. Instead, parents should avoid condemning statements and should provide opportunities for the child to have positive interactions with people of the racial background that the birthfather represents.

Inheritable Conditions

If potentially inheritable conditions, such as mental illness or mental limitations, are a part of your child's genetic history, you should convey the inheritability of the condition without frightening him. It is also important to relate the positive aspects of the situation, that even though the child may be at a greater risk for developing a certain condition, the chances are still in his favor that he will not, and that there are also risks in the general population.

Children can learn that there are services to help people who develop these conditions. They can understand that even if they do develop an inherited condition, they do not need to lead the same lives as their birthparents. The more honest and specific the information that parents offer their children, the better prepared the children will be to deal with it.

Children's Questions

One of your greatest challenges will be to help your child understand why this particular situation happened to him. Why was he the only child in a family of five to be singled out for abuse? Why did his birthmother leave him in a dumpster, his umbilical cord still attached? Will he repeat the same undesirable behaviors?

What parents can do is provide factual information, make neutral or positive inferences ("Sometimes parents don't know how to take proper care of their children"), affirm the children's feelings, and provide an opportunity for the children to grieve. For many children, therapeutic counseling is also necessary.

While it is still important to express hope and concern for your child's birthparents, it is as important to let him know that the adoptive relationship is a permanent one. Parents can say, "We hope that your birthfather is no longer using chemicals and is happy, but you are part of our family now and that part won't change." That response addresses concerns for the birthparent but answers the unspoken question of whether the child will go back once the birthparent's condition is changed.

Children who worry about whether they will be like their birthparents can be helped by parents emphasizing the children's positive traits in similar situations. To a child who was abused, it would be helpful for the parent to say, "You really take good care of your pets. You have learned how to care for animals and you do a good job. You are learning some of the skills that it takes to be a good parent." When children realize that they are learning and using the skills that their birthparents lacked, they can realize that they are not destined to repeat the actions of their birthparents.

Children are enormously resilient. With the help of their parents and positive interactions, they can face the pain of their past, accept their situation, and move on toward building a happy life with healthy relationships.

Guidelines for Disclosure

When the time is right to disclose difficult background information to children, parents should take care to:

- reveal factual information in carefully chosen terms that the children can understand;
- put the details of the situation in context as much as possible, so the story reflects the birthparents' reactions to their circumstances;
- stress that adults, not children, were responsible for these actions;
- include positive information about birth relatives and the efforts or choices they made to help, so the children can find sources of pride in their heritage and background;
- take time to discuss the situation with the children and encourage feedback about their feelings;
- help the children choose ways to incorporate strengths acquired from genetic relatives and avoid repeating their mistakes;
- encourage children to identify goals and supports for managing areas of vulnerability, such as impulsiveness or anger;
- use counseling or psychotherapy resources if appropriate;
- follow up on the conversation by asking children what they are thinking or feeling.

Part Five

~~~~~~

MANAGING RESOURCES

F amily preservation is as important for adoptive families as it is for biological families. Adoptive families, especially those with children with special issues, need affordable and accessible support services.

In many instances, resources are already in place to assist families. Although increased efforts have been made to make these services and information about them more available, no comprehensive information or referral system exists for parents. As a result, many of the services and benefits for eligible families go unused.

The task for parents is to fashion their own service strategy by planning and coordinating the resources they need for their children. Parents will need to educate themselves about the available resources and, in many cases, lobby for access to these services.

A growing number of adoption professionals see the investigation of post-adoption services such as these as important pursuits for adoptive parents. Traditionally, obstacles to parents using these services have been lack of information about the available services and parents' perceptions that the use of these services is indicative of poor parenting skills, greediness, or other motives.

It has finally become acceptable that parents are active advocates for children who cannot speak for themselves. Exploring every service option is an appropriate and responsible action for parents.

Sources of Help

Many organizations, some private agencies, and a number of state social service departments have provisions for post-adoption services. These programs can range from information about adoption subsidies and benefits to referrals for therapeutic counseling and residential placement to maintenance of adoption registries.

Adoptive parent support groups and organizations for children with special medical and emotional needs have proven to be very effective support systems for families and the basis for much successful legislation on behalf of adopted children.

Another resource that has been beneficial for adoptive families is special-issues play groups for children. Whether these groups are formed for children with ADD, children involved in open adoptions, or any other special issue, the friendships that the children make and share have proven to be very valuable. Frequently these groups are formed in conjunction with adoptive family support groups.

26

^^

SECURING SUBSIDIES

Adoptive parents need to think in terms of an overall plan of support for their children with special needs. Frequently this means combining a number of different subsidies for a fully comprehensive plan.

The Adoption Assistance and Child Welfare Act of 1980 is a federal law that makes financial assistance and other services available to children with special needs. Although this legislation enables families to adopt and parent children with excessive medical expenses, the benefit is frequently underused because parents are not aware that their children may be eligible for assistance.

The federal adoption subsidy program, *Title IV E*, matches funds with state government programs. It provides a monthly stipend, automatic Medicaid eligibility, and eligibility for Title XX social services. Another federal program covers nonrecurring expenses in adopting special-needs children.

Many states have state-funded programs that are subsidies intended to pay for services not covered by Medicaid or private health insurance plans. The chief use of this type of program is medical and mental health services. Children who are not eligible for Title IV E subsidies may be eligible for such a state program.

A growing number of states have post-adoption subsidies that can be accessed after finalization. These are generally state-only service subsidies that pay for medical or psychological services not covered by Medicaid or private health insurance.

Benefits are generally paid by the state from which the child was adopted. Some state-only subsidies are available for post-adoption services from the state of residence if it differs from the originating state. Copies of the state regulations are the best source of information on the availability of such programs.

Subsidies are paid directly to parents and are designed to help defray the cost of raising the child. Most states have standard payment rates and limitations on subsidy benefits. The amount of the monthly stipend varies by state and is frequently based on foster care rates in the state, the severity of the child's need, and the child's age, or a combination of those factors.

Eligibility Requirements

In order to be eligible for a subsidy, a child must be identified as having special needs. The definition of *special needs* varies from state to state but, in general, children are considered to have special needs if they are older (over two) when adopted, are adopted as part of a sibling group, are at high risk of developing disabilities, or have a medically verified mental, physical, or emotional disability.

Many adopted children who have been a part of the foster care system have emotional problems, such as attachment disorders or learning disabilities. These children may also be eligible for benefits.

Any child who meets the minimum requirements is eligible for benefits. The adoptive parents' income may not be considered as a determinant for eligibility, although it may affect the amount of the subsidy.

Negotiating and Accessing Subsidies

Subsidies are generally determined before an adoption is made final. They are put into effect through a written agreement that enumerates benefits and each party's responsibilities. Subsidies can be negotiated and can be individualized to cover current support as well as contingencies, such as counseling services if needed. They should be tailored to individual family needs and be as clear and descriptive as possible. Subsidies can be renegotiated at any time with mutual consent.

After your initial visits with a child before placement, review the child's records and speak with her social worker or foster care provider in order to obtain an idea of the child's medical needs and family background and the cost of services that she requires, has been receiving, and might need in the future. Also make sure you are informed of all the possible subsidy benefits to which she is entitled.

You may apply for a subsidy at any time; however, subsidies are easier to obtain before finalization. If you apply after placement, you may be required to provide proof of extenuating circumstances—that you had been uninformed or misinformed about the availability of benefits, the eligibility requirements, or the child's medical history or family background, for example. Once you have gained the right of reconsideration, you will still need to prove your child's eligibility.

States are not required to but may make retroactive payments, dating back either to the date of finalization or the date of placement. The states may be resistant to making retroactive payments; however, if you win an appeal for subsidy assistance after finalization, you may have a good case for retroactive payments.

The Adoption Assistance and Child Welfare Act of 1980 is widely misinterpreted and commonly violated by local policies and regulations. Parents frequently win subsidy decisions on appeal, especially decisions related to eligibility.

If you feel that your child may be eligible for benefits, ask your state adoption office for information about adoption subsidies and benefits in your state. The resources at the end of this key can provide information about subsidies and other benefits. The American Public Welfare Association, for example, provides a state-by-state breakdown of benefits. Your local adoption support group may also be a good source of information.

The Appeal Process

If your request for assistance is denied, whether the request is for eligibility for a program or for an increase in benefits, you may appeal the decision through the state's administrative fair hearing process.

Generally the hearing process is very sensitive to the needs of applicants. Attempts are made for the hearings to be accessible. They can often be requested by telephone, they can be scheduled to accommodate the convenience of the appealer, and every effort is made to help individuals state their cases without an attorney. Costs are very low, frequently free at the lower levels of appeal, and reasonable limits are maintained regarding the amount of time that can pass before a decision is made. A denial of an appeal must be communicated in writing and must provide information about the next step in the appeal process.

If your request is again denied, the next level of appeal is an administrative review of the hearing record. These are frequently conducted by a legal staff member in the state's department of human services.

A denial at this stage presents another opportunity for appeal—a judicial review, which is a petition to the local court for review of the case. This is the last stage in the appeal process and the step at which applicants frequently engage an attorney.

Subsidy Resources

Contact the following organizations for information and printed materials about adoption subsidies and benefits:

Adoptive Families of America
3333 Highway 100 North
Minneapolis, MN 55422
612-535-4829

The American Public Welfare Association
810 First Street NE, Suite 500
Washington, DC 20002-4267
202-682-0100

The National Adoption Assistance Training, Resource, and
    Information Network (NAATRIN)
800-470-6665

National Adoption Information Clearinghouse
11426 Rockville Pike, Suite 410
Rockville, MD 20852
301-231-6512

North American Council on Adoptable Children
970 Raymond Avenue, Suite 106
St. Paul, MN 55114-1149
612-644-3036

27

‸‸‸

FINDING AN EFFECTIVE THERAPIST

T he vast majority of adoptive families weather the ups and downs of family development without professional mental health services. For some children and some families, however, there are circumstances that suggest a need for more than what the normal loving home can provide. For these families, the assistance of a mental health therapist can be beneficial.

The choice of an appropriate mental health professional is so important, especially for adopted children who may already have faced great losses, that parents need to carefully choose the specialists who will work with their children. If you think the services of a mental health professional might be beneficial, a good time to begin looking is now, before a crisis happens.

Early preparation is especially important for parents adopting a child with serious behavior problems. These parents should expect further behavior problems and repeated crisis situations and should initiate family counseling from the outset.

Recognizing Stresses

If your child is forming strong relationships with peers and adults, becoming confident and secure, and learning skills appropriate for his age, you can feel comfortable that he is developing appropriately. If, on the other hand, he exhibits behaviors such as anxiety, fearfulness, depression, anger, hostility, impulsiveness, lack of control, or lack of an ability to find success, his developmental process is being interrupted and he might benefit from assistance from a mental health professional.

If you are unsure about your child's development, ask for input from professionals who regularly interact with your child—his teacher or his pediatrician, for example. They can compare his development with a large group of children his age and determine whether or not his behaviors seem balanced.

Modern theory suggests that if stress-related behaviors are beginning to be noticeable and are interfering with a child's normal development, parents should contact a therapist much as they would visit their family physician for treatment of a sore throat—that is, to seek help for the specific symptoms or behaviors—and cease treatment when the undesirable behaviors subside.

Qualities of an Effective Therapist

Many professionals recommend that adoptive parents find a well-qualified mental health specialist who has expertise in adoption issues, rather than an adoption specialist who has some expertise in mental health services. Commonly, licensed mental health providers are psychiatrists, psychologists, licensed social workers, licensed clinical social workers with supervised experience in doing therapy, marriage and family therapists, and some mental health nurses.

The therapist you choose needs to have credentials and expertise. In addition, he needs to have some personal qualities that make him the type of person with whom you can work. An effective therapist must be warm and human.

152

Above all he should be nonpossessive. He is there to help you, not to parent your child or to have all the answers.

Your therapist also needs to have a measure of flexibility so that he can suit his therapies to the behaviors and needs of your child. These behaviors may change over the course of your relationship with the therapist, and he needs to have the flexibility to accommodate different needs.

There are a variety of counseling theories, or approaches, that a therapist might use. Behavior modification, play therapy, and psychoanalysis are examples of different approaches. Finding just the right match between the therapist, the approach, and the client is important. You and your child will be more comfortable with some approaches than with others.

If your child has serious behavior problems, therapies intended to change behavior rather than offer the child opportunities for introspection are recommended. The therapist may use somewhat unconventional methods, including observing the child in the home and providing parents with specific techniques for dealing with the child's undesirable behaviors. This approach is frequently popular with parents and unpopular with children. Parents like the approach because results come quickly; children tend to dislike the approach because they do not have the opportunity to avoid facing the consequences of their behaviors.

Clarifying Expectations
Parents need to decide what they would like to gain from the counseling experience and communicate that goal to their children's therapists. Children also need to be told the truth about the reasons for therapy and what the therapy is expected to accomplish. A context that implies that the family needs some help to understand what is happening in order to make things better for the child lifts the burden

from the child and represents shared responsibilities and positive goals for change.

The therapist needs to indicate the structure and the ground rules that parents can expect from the relationship, including:

- the diagnostic procedures to be used,
- a plan of therapy,
- the estimated duration of treatment,
- the expected benefits,
- the rules of confidentiality and communication,
- the associated risks, and
- the availability of emergency access.

Good, clear communication between therapists and parents helps ensure effective treatment for children. For adopted children especially, parents need to make every effort to preserve an alliance with their children's therapists. The issue of broken relationships is a fragile area for many adopted children. Both the hiring and the firing of a therapist need to be done with great caution and with attention to the implications about the meaning of the relationship to the children.

Formulating a Plan

You need to be the case manager in planning and coordinating the services you need for your child. If he needs a play group for certain issues and a behavior specialist for other issues, you should establish the details of a program that is tailored for his needs.

Frequently, varied approaches that include some individual therapy, some family therapy, and some group therapy are effective. The advantage of a varied approach is that responsibility for the difficulties is shared by all of the participants, so difficult behaviors are not just the child's issues but also a challenge for the whole family. One such approach might be individual counseling for an adolescent, occasional family counseling for the child and his family, and group counseling for parents of a number of troubled teens. Regardless of the exact design, the most successful plan will be one that is a partnership between the therapist, the child, and the family.

Choosing a Therapist

An effective adoption therapist may be the key to your child's healthy transition to permanent placement now and his transition to independence later on. The time you take in identifying just the right professional for your child is time well spent.

As you begin your search for a therapist, ask for suggestions from your adoption professional and the adoptive parents' group in your area.

Considerations in Choosing a Therapist

- Experience with children and with adoption issues
- Professional approach
- Feelings about adoption as a positive option
- Cost
- Location
- Insurance or payment plans accepted
- The availability of sliding scale fees
- The recommended length and frequency of counseling sessions

When deciding if a particular therapist is right for your family, schedule an initial interview to discuss your family's particular needs. Some professionals provide an initial interview at no cost; others charge for the service.

28

‸‸

EASING A DISRUPTING ADOPTION

Despite the best intentions and preparation to parent adopted children, it does happen that terminations occur and the children are returned to the adoption agencies. Technically, the term *disruption* is used to describe an adoption that is terminated before finalization, and *dissolution* describes an adoption that is terminated after finalization. Since a termination disrupts both adopted children and their families, *disruption* is commonly used to describe the process whenever it occurs.

Estimates vary about the frequency of adoption disruptions, but they tend to be more frequent among older-child adoptions—particularly with those children who have experienced multiple placements—and relatively uncommon among infant adoptions.

Solutions are available that, although they may not eliminate disruptions altogether, have a good chance of reducing the number of terminations, and making those terminations that do occur easier for children.

The best solution, of course, is prevention. Successful prevention happens when both parents and children receive adequate and accurate information and preparation about what to expect from the adoption experience. While access to this information is important in all adoptive placements, it is critically important for families adopting children who have a history of multiple moves, who have previously experienced an adoption disruption, or who have other high-risk adoption factors present.

The next best solution is successful intervention, including respite care or residential treatment, if necessary, before problems escalate to the point that continuation of the placement is not possible. If intervention is not effective and the decision is made to disrupt, great care must be taken in easing the child out of placement.

When adoptions reach the stage of disruption, it is often caused by a disparity in expectations: the parent expects something the child cannot give or the child gives something the parent did not expect. The cause is generally attributed to four factors that may or may not be present in individual cases: (1) incomplete or incorrect information is provided to adopters, often by adoption workers eager to make a placement, (2) the stresses of adoption, (3) the child's traumatic history of abuse and broken attachments, or (4) unforeseeable circumstances, such as catastrophic hardships or the death of a parent.

Prevention

Adopted children benefit when their parents have complete information about the children's background. Knowledge of this information is even more important if children have special adoption risks that place them at a higher risk of disruption. When parents have information about early stresses or potential risks and the behaviors that the children have exhibited or might be expected to exhibit, they are better prepared to help their children cope and to possibly deflect some of the devastating effects of the children's prior traumas.

Two very successful activities for families who adopt children at risk for disruption are establishing a buddy system with another, experienced family that has adopted a child with similar needs and behaviors, and working as a family to create a significant life book for the child.

Parents of children who exhibit extreme behaviors need to know in straightforward terms what to expect—that the children may be likely to set fires or terrorize playmates, for example. Equally important for parents is preparedness for the ways the children's behaviors may affect the dynamics of the family and the individuals within the family.

Successful prevention also requires preparedness for any children who are at a higher risk of disruption. Such children's introduction to permanent placement needs to be gradual whenever possible and, for children beyond infancy, paired with an explanation of what to expect. Children at risk of disruption will benefit from:

- time to adjust to the idea of permanent placement,
- instruction about how people form new relationships and how they adjust to new living arrangements,
- information about the new families and their lifestyles and what their expectations will be, and
- an opportunity to say good-bye to important people.

Children and parents also need to be prepared for the possibility of disruption. For children, this preparation helps them understand that not all situations are right for all children. If a disruption were to occur, it would mean that the situation was not right for the child, not that the child or family was at fault. If a situation becomes irreversible, the primary concern of parents must be to ease the process for the child rather than demanding an abrupt and immediate removal of the child from the home.

Identifying parental responsibility for a smooth transition serves two purposes: (1) it illuminates the importance of safeguarding the children's feelings during disruption, and (2) it prompts parents to think about prevention rather than reaction to crisis situations. This may mean that parents pursue a number of plans—from seeking early interventions to lining up emergency families to take the children until crises subside—before irreversible situations develop.

Early Stages of Difficulty

Families will show somewhat predictable indicators that point toward disruption. These include:

- noticeable family discomfort that does not subside over time,
- increased discord,
- out-of-proportion complaints about the children's undesirable behaviors or the overall situation,
- a period of tranquillity without evidence of resolution of the conflict,
- return of turmoil and conflicts that lead to a crisis, and
- the decision to disrupt the adoption.

If these stages are interrupted by interventions from mental health specialists trained in adoption issues, families have a chance of successfully preventing a disruption. Sometimes professional therapeutic interventions point to the need for short-term respite care or longer-term residential treatment for the children, approaches that have been proven to be very effective for some children.

Parents tend to begin thinking about disruption when they sense that the children's behaviors are having detrimental effects on other children in the family. Another internal pressure point is the relationship between parenting partners. Too often, though, families do not seek professional assistance until the cycle of conflict has escalated to a point that makes a reversal unlikely.

Easing Children Out of Placement

When parents take responsibility in easing the termination procedure for their children, they convey their love and concern for the children and their interest in helping them find the situations that will help them. Children facing adoption disruption need their parents to tell them what is happening in terms that do not assess blame. The children also need time to say good-bye to important people in their lives and make a gradual move out of the home.

Parents can say, "We care about you and want you to be happy. We found out that we aren't as understanding as we thought we could be. We feel scared when you get angry and hurt others. Perhaps you can find another family that is more understanding, or you can learn different ways to express your anger."

Children benefit when their parents help them with scripts to tell the important people in their lives what is happening. A child could appropriately tell her teachers and friends that she is moving to a new situation where she can get more help with some important issues in her life, for example.

Photographs of the home and family members should also be provided for children who are facing disruption. Even if the children do not appear to want them, they should have these records of the time that they spent with the family. Their case workers can keep the photos for the children's life books.

Children have a right to a gradual transition out of the home. Their move out should be neither immediate nor abrupt. If necessary, emergency plans can be implemented in the event of a crisis situation. After reactions to the crisis behaviors have subsided, the children should be permitted to return home to continue with the disruption plans.

After the children leave, parents usually expect to feel relief. The more common emotion is grief and then feelings of anger or blame. Parents' anger may be directed toward the agencies for not providing sufficient information or support, the children for exhibiting the disrupting behaviors, the therapists for not curing the problems, and each other for failure to overcome the difficulties of the situation.

If other children reside in the home, they need to understand that it was the situation that was wrong rather than specific people. Other adopted children need to be reassured that they will not have to leave also, that staying is not contingent on good behavior.

29

ACCESSING BIRTH
RECORDS

With the move toward more open communication between birth and adoptive parents, the question of a search for information about an adopted person's background or to initiate contact with birth relatives is not as emotionally charged as it once was, when the majority of adoption records were sealed.

For children who lack personal background information, the idea of a search continues to carry weighty issues for both the adopted persons and their birth and adoptive relatives. Balanced against the right of every person to have direct, personal knowledge about his genetic heritage is the right to privacy that birthparents assumed when they made the original plan for adoption, and the perceived threat of divided loyalties that adoptive parents may fear.

While the controversy continues, societal changes are being made that allow adopted persons and birthparents a say in the availability of access to records. This important move—one that allows the input of key people rather than the whims of records clerks or the regulations of adoption agencies—is an important step forward.

One such attempt at a solution involves a court-sponsored path to birth family meetings. Legislation in some states permits a birthparent or adopted person to petition county probate courts for a confidential intermediary to be appointed. The intermediary is authorized to search the official records, contact birth family members, and inquire if they are willing to meet.

Finding birthparents—either by making direct contact or by locating more information about their personal histories—can be an enormous relief to adopted persons. A search can be a good opportunity for parents to work together with their children to help them put together some missing pieces about their lives or to enhance the lives that they already lead. Parents who support their children in a search and facilitate the locating of information often find an opportunity to develop even more intimacy with their children.

Reasons for Searching

Many adopted persons report that they conduct a search for two reasons: (1) to find someone who looks like them, and (2) to reassure their birthparents that the decision was a good one, that they were placed with loving parents, and that life turned out to be good for them.

Those who do actively search are not so much troubled as they are curious; they feel a need to look backward before they can move forward. Some people feel compelled to do a search at a certain point in their life—as they get older, as they experience the birth of their children, or as they watch their parents get older, for example. Adopted persons with no interest in searching often have children who are interested in finding out more about themselves and their genetic origins.

Most adopted persons at one point or another in their lives do carry on a personal, intra-psychic search for information about their background. For many this is limited to curiosity and fantasy about their birthparents, the reasons for placement, and conjecture about what life would have been like had their birthparents been able to raise them. Very few adopted persons actually take the next step to mounting an active search to obtain information or to establish a relationship with their birth families.

Emotional Readiness

Adopted persons who search hope for a happy ending to their quest for information. Because of the sensitivity of the situation and the fact that, in many cases, an adoption may be years old, searchers need to prepare themselves emotionally for varying disappointments, such as the following:

* closed (sealed) or nonexistent records,
* an expensive and time-consuming search that leads to no additional information,
* resentment from the adoptive parents toward the adopted person's interest in the search,
* discovery of negative information,
* disapproval of the search on the part of the birthparents,
* death of the birthparents,
* birthparents' request for financial support,
* denial of parentage, or
* differences in expectations between the adopted persons and their birthparents about ongoing relationships.

Despite the very real possibility for disappointment, adopted adults who search often report a sense of tranquillity that comes from the initiation of the search itself rather than from any positive outcomes. Adopted people, who have experienced the most basic loss of control over their destiny, are frequently satisfied with the process of the search itself, content that they have taken an active part in attempting to discover the missing parts of their existence.

Searchers need to be keenly aware of the emotional impact that sudden contact can have on the lives of the people for whom they search. Birthparents may have fully expected their confidentiality to be maintained; they may not have revealed the fact of the adoption to significant people in their lives or, in the case of birthfathers, may not even have been aware of the existence of children. An unexpected phone call or face-to-face meeting could be very unnerving for everyone involved. To offset the potential for surprise, searchers may wish to seek the assistance of a confidential intermediary to contact birth family members and ask if they are willing to meet.

Professional vs. Informal Searches

Searches can be conducted by professional researchers or by adopted persons or their relatives. Adoption support groups, some geared specifically toward helping birthparents and grown-up adopted persons search each other out, exist across the United States and Canada and can assist an adopted person in locating information domestically or internationally.

Information about adoptive searches is also available through computerized on-line services. Forums on genealogy, adoption, or history and informal chats among people interested in adoption are popular sources of information and support.

Professional researchers have the advantage of a proven track record and established contacts in key positions. Fees vary but generally include charges for the researcher's time and expenses—none of which may result in contact with the person or persons being sought.

The advantage of the adopted person conducting the search himself is that he may stop or slow down the search any time he feels uncomfortable. He may be satisfied with obtaining information such as the hometown or occupation of his birthparents, rather than actual identifying information about the person for whom he is searching.

165

Despite the difficulties inherent in adoptive searches, many adopted persons have been successful in locating their birthparents.

Meeting and Aftermath

Most adult adopted persons are not searching for an additional set of parents. They already have parents who love them. Adults who search frequently report that they are looking to find a physical resemblance or to find answers to questions about either their genetic histories or the reasons for adoptive placement.

Many searchers fear the rejection they may encounter if they are successful in locating and contacting birth relatives; however, the vast majority who are successful report overwhelming acceptance by their birth relatives. For the searchers, this unexpected acceptance brings forth unanticipated feelings of conflict between euphoria over the newly discovered relatives and fear of the perception of having betrayed their adoptive parents.

The duration of biological relative/placed child relationships following successful searches has been shown to be somewhat limited, however. The combination of the completed exchange of background information and changes in the interests and responsibilities of the people involved tends to limit these relationships to a matter of a few years.

Organizations for Searchers

Adopted Teen Connection
P.O. Box 16567
Phoenix, AZ 85011

AID (Adoptees Identity Discovery)
Box 2159
Sunnyvale, CA 94087
408-737-2222

ALMA (Adoptees Liberty Movement Assn.)
P.O. Box 727
Radio City Station
New York, NY 10101-8727
212-581-1568

American Adoption Congress
P.O. Box 23641
Washington, DC 20024
212-988-0110

CUB (Concerned United Birthparents)
2000 Walker Street
Des Moines, IA 50317
515-262-9120, 515-225-6497

International Soundex Reunion Registry
P.O. Box 2312
Carson City, NV 89702
702-882-6270

TSIA (Truth Seekers in Adoption)
Box 366
Prospect Heights, IL 60070-0366
312-625-4476

30

~~~~~~

THE PASSAGE TO ADULTHOOD

The hope is, of course, that by adulthood, adopted persons have reached an equilibrium about their status as adopted individuals in society and are ready for independence.

The passage to adulthood is easier for some adopted children than for others, though. Whereas the majority of children move rather smoothly from childhood to adolescence to independence, others are not ready for the move out of the family at the time that society, and frequently their families, expect them to depart. Obviously this disparity of readiness can be a major cause of turmoil in a family.

Leaving Home

Some children who are never able to bond successfully leave their families early, often as runaways or to long-term residential treatment. Other children may be reluctant to leave. The idea of independence may be very scary to them. These children may not be emotionally ready to separate from their families, or they may not have adequate life skills to live independently. For children who have experienced multiple broken relationships, for example, the idea of another separation may be very difficult.

The customary transition time for children to leave home and begin independent living is graduation from high school. As parents, we hope that we will have provided our children with sufficient skills to tackle the challenges ahead. For many children, this is indeed the case and the children leave home headed for college, a job, military service, or vocational training. For others, especially children who have difficulties that have delayed their development, the path to the future may also be somewhat delayed.

Parents may need to set aside some of their expectations about the transition from the home to independence to allow for individual differences in their children's readiness for departure from the family. Sometimes children just need maturity. Sometimes parents just need to let go.

Most children will eventually make a successful transition and form lives as productive citizens. Others will not. Parents of children who never successfully adjust cannot blame themselves for decisions that their children make as adults. They can keep the door open for children who want to change and, hopefully, they can find contentment in the knowledge that even in a small way they had a positive impact on the lives of their children.

Young Adulthood

Life changes for young adults are likely to cause adopted persons to revisit adoption issues that they may have thought were long since resolved. Typically, young adulthood is the time when most adopted persons search for either their biological relatives or answers to previously unanswered questions. The trigger to the initiation of their search is frequently a significant life event: marriage, the birth of children, or the death of one or both adoptive parents.

The prospect of intimacy and parenthood reawakens adoption issues, such as a search for a genetic connection. The anticipation of parenthood spurs a look to the past as well as to the future. When the new parent is an adopted person, the universal urge to avoid the mistakes of one's own parents becomes an attempt to avoid the mistakes of both biological and adoptive parents. For many, a focus on the genetic resemblance to the child, especially a physical resemblance, reawakens adoption issues when the adopted person is looking forward to knowing another person in the universe who looks like her.

Middle Age

For most people in their forties and fifties, life has brought career choices, a family, and regular doses of success and failure. At this stage, many adults are beginning to think about the legacy they will leave behind, whether through their children or through contributions to society. With the emotional sense that the clock is ticking, adult adopted persons who have ignored issues related to adoption up until this point may feel as if it is time for them to take action and resolve some previously unresolved questions before it is too late.

This growing sense of urgency about the future spurs an interest in some adopted persons to reexamine the past, so they can pass on their own history to the next generation. They may also fear the death of their biological relatives and the information that would die with them.

Old Age

The move to old age tends to bring about an examination of life and a determination of whether, in the end, the life was worth living. When a search is conducted during old age, the purpose is generally an attempt at bringing to a conclusion the issues that had gnawed at the adopted person her whole life. Predictably, many of the key birth relatives are long since deceased and the memories of others, long since dimmed. For those who search in old age, the goal may be one last attempt at linkage to humanity, no matter how tenuous that link might be.

Successful Resolution

Adult adopted persons who succeed at resolving their adoption portion of life's issues have two overwhelmingly similar characteristics: (1) sufficient life experiences to understand that choices are not always black-and-white issues, and (2) the capacity to forgive. Understanding and forgiveness allow adopted persons to comprehend the conditions that resulted in their adoptive placement and to accept the strengths and weaknesses of all the members of their own adoption circle—their birthparents, their adoptive parents, and themselves.

Family Bonds

On the eve of her son's high school graduation, one mother who had been through the normal ups and downs of child-rearing was overheard to say, "I can't remember how we got from where we were to where we are—but I know I enjoyed the trip!" Perhaps that statement describes the process for adoptive parents as well as for their children who journey to adulthood. The details may fade as the years go by, but there is contentment in discovering that, indeed, there was joy in the journey.

171

QUESTIONS AND ANSWERS

We have a newly adopted infant daughter whose birth-parents are very young. After learning more about the benefits of open adoptions, we would like to establish contact with our daughter's birthparents, but neither her birthfather nor birthmother has any interest. Is there anything we can do?

It is not uncommon for adoptive parents to feel more comfortable about openness than birthparents do. In fact, as time passes, adoptive parents tend to desire more contact, while the birthparents' desire for contact tends to decrease. It may help for you to talk with the birthparents privately about your interest in establishing contact. You can explain that their situation may change in the next few years and that if they would ever like to reestablish a relationship, your door and your heart will be open to them.

Give them your name, phone number, and address and tell them that if you move you will send them the new address. Right now your child's birthparents may have no idea of what their role could conceivably be in your family's life. Possibly they will reenter the picture in four or five years. In the meantime, it may help to make sure that each birthparent gets his own copy of photos of your child.

I feel a need to bend over backward to include my son's birthparents in our family activities, and to be a super parent for my child based on anxiety about what his birthparents will think of my parenting skills. I'm exhausting myself physically and emotionally. Is there a better approach?

Treat your child's birthparents exactly like family. Do you bend over backward to include other family members?

Your relationship with your child should be filled with joy. Parenting by guilt robs your child of the opportunity to enjoy the parent-child relationship with you, and he will sense the stress that you are experiencing. You must feel joyful about your child's extended family if you want your child to feel joyful. Your job is not to see that your son's birthparents' needs are met but that your son's needs are met.

When in doubt about dealings with birthparents, ask yourself, "How would I react if this were my (sister, family friend, brother-in-law)?" Then treat the child's birthparent in the same manner.

My daughter, whom I adopted as an eighteen month old from Thailand, is ambivalently attached. Whether we are in the doctor's waiting room or at a fast-food restaurant, she will go to a stranger and be perfectly charming. My efforts to restrain her are met with glares and screams from the child and stares from the adults she has befriended. I have lived with the embarrassment of this type of situation for two years now. What can I do about it?

The choice of your actions needs to be based on what makes you feel okay in parenting your child. Although this behavior is chronic, you need to treat it like any other temper

173

tantrum and, incidentally, with the same techniques you use at home.

One strategy might be to say to the child loudly enough for others to hear, "You are having a temper tantrum. You need to calm down." A controlled response such as this indicates that you are choosing to act in a controlled manner rather than reacting to the child's uncontrolled behaviors.

For help with coping with this and other behaviors of ambivalently attached children, you might benefit from access to a support group in which other parents of ambivalently attached children can share their experiences and suggestions.

Remember, too, that you do not go into a fast-food restaurant to form lasting relationships. Reinforcing consequences for your children's inappropriate behaviors is more important than any embarrassment you might experience.

I have a transracially adopted child. Should I move to a neighborhood more consistent with her ethnic background?

Generally speaking, transracially adopted children do better when they live in a neighborhood that is either ethnically mixed or consistent with the child's ethnic background. If no such neighborhoods exist or if a move is impractical, strive to expose your child to information about her ethnicity and introduce her to other children (preferably adopted children) of her ethnic background.

It is also important that you demonstrate acceptance of others by developing friendships with people of various ethnicities. You can, for example, attend church services and festivals where your child can encounter people with similar backgrounds.

My child was abandoned as an infant, so I truly do not have any information about his background. How can I help him with his questions about his heritage, who he is, and where he came from?

Start now to record any information that you may have about your child. Obtain all the information that the agency can provide, including the time, location, and approximate age when your child was found, the personnel on duty at the adoption agency, and any official reports, including police records or newspaper accounts relevant to your child's discovery. Even if you are never able to obtain information that leads to a meeting with any family members, your child may be happy to have information about the locale of his birth.

Frequently people who know that my daughter was adopted comment on how we look alike. I feel that they are trying to deny the importance of our biological differences by overemphasizing the physical similarities. How should I respond?

Remember that your most important response is one that reaffirms your child's belongingness in your family. Your response can be the same whether or not the speaker knows that your child was adopted—"Yes, isn't it neat that we fit."

Later you can tell your daughter, "Isn't it interesting that your origins are in Mexico and mine are in Ireland, and people see the resemblances between the races."

GLOSSARY

Adoption Assistance and Child Welfare Act of 1980 a federal law that makes financial assistance and other services available to children with special needs

Adoption circle key members of an adoption unit: birthparents, adoptive parents, and adopted persons

Adoption issues common issues of isolation, a search for self, and a sense of a lost past and lost relationships that adopted persons frequently experience

Adoption registry a data bank with records of identifying information related to people involved in an adoptive placement

Adoption risk factors circumstances such as a history of abuse or multiple moves that may serve to jeopardize successful adoptive placement for a child

Ambivalent attachment an attachment disorder characterized by indiscriminate shows of affection, such as charm to strangers and open hostility to parents

Attachment mutual love and affection between parent and child

Attachment disorder a condition that interferes with a child's ability to develop reciprocal feelings of love and caring with parents and siblings

Attention Deficit Disorder (ADD) a persistent pattern of inattention and/or hyperactivity-impulsivity-hypoactivity that is more frequent and severe than is typically observed in people at a comparable level of development

Biologically built family a family in which the child(ren) has been biologically conceived by both parents

Birthparents the set of parents who conceived a child

Black any child of primarily African descent

Blended family a family built with children who join the family through any combination of birth, adoption, and/or step-relationships

Bonding the development of a close parent-child relationship; the trust that the child has in the parent that the parent will meet the child's needs

Caucasian any white child of European, North African, or southwest Asian ancestry

Childhood depression an emotional condition characterized by extreme behaviors such as anger, hostility, or lack of motivation that is thought to be associated with the losses of adoption, particularly in older children

Child of color any child of African, Hispanic, Native American, East Indian and/or Asian descent

Claiming the process of identifying ways that children are like their parents

Confidential adoption an adoption of a child between anonymous birthparents and adopters in which, generally, little or no background information about the child is available

Confidential intermediary a court-appointed authority empowered to search official adoption records, contact birth family members, and inquire if they are willing to meet

Cultural heritage the set of customs, traditions, language, and, frequently, religion that is shared by a large group of people

Cultural openness a process that encourages the exploration of cultural rather than biological roots and the sharing of personal friendships with others of a similar background

Disruption an interruption to the adoption process in which the adoption is terminated before it becomes final

177

Dissolution an interruption to the adoption process in which the adoption is terminated after it becomes final

Domestic adoption an adoption of a child who is a citizen of the United States

Entitlement a parent's feeling of being a rightful provider of love, guidance, and care to a child; a feeling of belonging

Ethnic heritage the traditions of biological ancestors as distinguished by common customs, mannerisms, language, and so on

Ethnicity common bonds of shared traditions among groups of people often based on regionalism, nationalism, or ancestry

Fantasy child the fanciful image of a perfect child, usually a child that embodies the most desirable traits of each parent

Fetal Alcohol Syndrome (FAS) a birth defect associated with heavy alcohol consumption in pregnant women that results in behavioral and physical abnormalities in children

Fetal Alcohol Effect (FAE) a less severe form of birth defect associated with alcohol consumption in pregnant women; similar to fetal alcohol syndrome but without the physical abnormalities

Genetic connection a biological relationship

Genetic heritage biological programming that children inherit from their birth ancestors

Goodness of fit a feeling of belonging in a family based on similarities of physical characteristics, values, interests, or personalities, or all of these

Inherited traits inborn characteristics that are attributed to genetic programming

Interim care temporary residential custodial care of a child in a nonrelated family setting

International children children who are not citizens of the United States

International adoption the legal adoption of children who are not U. S. citizens

Interracial children children of mixed racial heritage

Life book a scrapbook-type collection of photographs, drawings, and keepsakes that helps an adopted child link his life before and after adoption

Minority children children who belong to a racial minority, usually children who are raised in a predominant culture other than their own

Nonidentifying contact interaction between birth and adoptive parents in which identifying information is not shared

Open adoption a style of adoption that is characterized by full disclosure of identifying information and an agreement to maintain ongoing contact between birth and adoptive parents

Orphanage a group home intended to house homeless or abandoned children

Permanence an opportunity for a child to establish a long-lasting relationship as part of a family unit

Personal story a factual, accurate account of the circumstances related to a child's birth and placement

Play group a support system for children who have mutual interests or experiences and that allows opportunities for play and fellowship

Positive Adoption Language (PAL) nonjudgmental terminology that emphasizes the positive aspects of adoption as a method of family building

Race a major biological division of mankind as distinguished by common physical features

Respite care short-term care for children; an intervention that is intended to provide temporary relief for children and families

Residential placement a long-term group living arrangement often used as a therapeutic intervention plan for children with emotional or behavioral difficulties

Search the process of seeking information about a person's genetic heritage that may or may not involve actual contact with biological relatives

Semi-open adoption a style of adoption that involves the sharing of information (usually nonidentifying) between birth and adoptive parents through an intermediary

Siblings legal brothers and sisters

Special-needs children generally, children who are older (over two) when adopted, are adopted as part of a sibling group, are at high risk of developing disabilities, or have a medically verified mental, physical, or emotional disability

Subsidies financial assistance provided by federal or state government that is intended to help offset ongoing expenses in caring for special-needs children

Support group a formal or informal group of people with common interests who share information, advice, and support

Termination the legal disruption of an adoption either before or after the adoption has been completed

Transcultural adoption adoption in which the adopted child has a cultural heritage that differs from that of the adoptive parents

Transracial adoption adoption in which the race of the adopted child differs from that of the adoptive parents

SUGGESTED READING

Resources for Adoptive Parents

Alexander, Shoshana. *In Praise of Single Parents: Mothers and Fathers Embracing the Challenge.* New York: Houghton Mifflin, 1994.

Benson, Peter L., Ph.D., Sharma, Anu R., Ph.D., and Roehlkepartain, Eugene C. *Growing Up Adopted.* Minneapolis: Search Institute, 1994

Bothun, Linda. *When Friends Ask About Adoption.* Chevy Chase, MD: Swan Publications, 1987.

Brodzinsky, David M., Ph.D., Schechter, Marshall D., M.D., and Henig, Robin Marantz. *Being Adopted: The Lifelong Search for Self.* New York: Anchor Books, 1992.

Combs, Allan. *Synchronicity.* New York: Shooting Star Press, 1994.

Delaney, Richard J. and Kunstal, Frank R. *Troubled Transplants: Unconventional Strategies for Helping Disturbed Foster & Adoptive Children.* Portland, ME: University of Southern Maine, 1993.

Doft, Norma. *When Your Child Needs Help: A Parent's Guide to Therapy for Children.* New York: Crown Publishing, 1994.

Hopson, Dr. Darlene Powell and Hopson, Dr. Derek S. *Raising the Rainbow Generation: Teaching Your Children to Be Successful in a Multicultural Society.* New York: Simon & Schuster, 1993.

McNamara, Barry E., Ed.D. and McNamara, Francine J., MSW, CSW. *Keys to Parenting a Child with Attention Deficit Disorder.* Hauppauge, NY: Barron's Educational Series, 1993.

McNamara, Joan and McNamara, Bernard, eds. *Adoption and the Sexually Abused Child.* Portland, ME: University of Southern Maine, 1990.

Melina, Lois Ruskai. *Raising Adopted Children*. New York: Solstice Press, 1986.

Sandmeyer, Marian. *When Love Is Not Enough: How Mental Health Professionals Can Help Special Needs Adoptive Families*. Washington, DC: Child Welfare League, 1988.

Schaffer, Judith and Lindstrom, Christina. *How to Raise an Adopted Child*. New York: Penguin Books, 1991.

Silber, Kathleen and Speedlin, Phylis. *Dear Birthmother: Thank You for Our Baby*. San Antonio, TX: Corona Publishing, 1991.

van Gulden, Holly and Bartels-Rabb, Lisa M. *Real Parents, Real Children*. New York: Crossroad, 1993.

Watkins, Mary and Fisher, Susan. *Talking with Young Children About Adoption*. New Haven, CT: Yale University Press, 1993.

On Living in an Adoptive Family

Askin, Jayne. *Search: A Handbook for Adoptees and Birthparents*. New York: Harper & Row, 1992.

Krementz, Jill. *How It Feels to Be Adopted*. New York: Alfred A. Knopf, 1982 (for teens).

Melina, Lois Ruskai. *Making Sense of Adoption: A Parent's Guide*. New York: HarperCollins, 1989.

Rosenberg, Maxine. *Growing Up Adopted*. New York: Bradbury Press, 1989 (for teens).

Sanford, Doris. *Loveletters: Responding to Children in Pain*. Sisters, OR: Questar Publishing, 1994.

—— *Don't Make Me Go Back, Mommy*. Sisters, OR: Questar Publishing, 1990.

Books for Children

Angelou, Maya. *My Painted House, My Friendly Chicken, and Me*. New York: Crown Publishing, 1994 (ages 4–10).

Brodzinsky, Anne Braff. *The Mulberry Bird*. Indianapolis: Perspectives Press, 1986 (ages 5–10).

Brunin, Catherine and Brunin, Sherry. *Is That Your Sister? A True Story of Adoption*. New York: Pantheon, 1992 (ages 2–10).

Freudberg, Judy and Geiss, Tony. *Susan and Gordon Adopt a Baby*. New York: Random House, 1992 (ages 3–8).

Joosse, Barbara M. *Mama, Do You Love Me?* San Francisco: Chronicle Books, 1991 (ages 2–7).

Kasza, Keiko. *A Mother for Choco*. New York: G. P. Putnam's Sons, 1992 (ages 2–8).

Koehler, Phoebe. *The Day We Met You*. New York: Macmillan Children's Books, 1990 (ages 1–5).

MacFarlane, Kee and Cunningham, Carolyn. *Steps to Healthy Touching*. Mount Dora, FL: Kidsrights, 1988 (age 5+).

Meyer, D. J., Vadascy, P. F., and Kewell, R. R. *Living with a Brother or Sister with Special Needs*. Seattle: University of Washington Press, 1985 (ages 8–13).

Miller, Kathryn Ann. *Did My First Mother Love Me?* Buena Park, CA: Morning Glory Press, 1994 (ages 4–8).

Special Resources

Culture Camps, Ethnic Reunions, Motherland Visits:

See Calendar of Events, *Adoptive Families* magazine, Adoptive Families of America, 3333 Highway 100 North, Minneapolis, MN 55422, 1-800-372-3300.

Multicultural Dolls:

Asian, African American, Native American, Latin American, and Hispanic baby dolls, toddler dolls, and fashion dolls and clothing. Ask for catalog. Adoptive Families of America, 3333 Highway 100 North, Minneapolis, MN 55422, 1-800-372-3300.

For siblings of people with disabilities:

The Sibling Information Network Newsletter, Sibling Information Network, The A. J. Pappanikou Center on Special Educational Rehabilitation, 991 Main Street, East Hartford, CT 06108.

Appendix A

^^

ADOPTIVE PARENTING ORGANIZATIONS

Adoptive Families of America
information and support for adoptive families
Adoptive Families magazine
3333 Highway 100 North
Minneapolis, MN 55422
612-535-4829;
Fax 612-535-7808
800-372-3300

American Adoption Congress
information for searching adult adoptees and birthparents
Box 44040
L'Enfant Plaza Station
Washington, DC 20026

Committee for Single Adoptive Parents
The Handbook for Single Adoptive Parents
Box 15084
Chevy Chase, MD 20825
202-966-6367

National Adoption Information Clearinghouse
wide range of free or inexpensive information
11426 Rockville Pike
Suite 410
Rockville, MD 20852
301-231-6512

North American Council on Adoptable Children
advocates for waiting children;
Adoptalk magazine
970 Raymond Avenue,
Suite 106
St. Paul, MN 55114-1149
612-644-3036;
Fax 612-644-9848

Single Parents Adopting Children Everywhere (SPACE)
single adoptive parent
  support group
6 Sunshine Avenue
Natick, MA 01760
508-655-5426

Single Parents With Adopted Kids
4116 Washington Road,
  Suite 202
Kenosha, WI 53144-1515
414-654-0629

CANADA

Adoption Council of Canada
information and education
  services
Box 8442 Stn. T
Ottawa, Ontario K1G 3H8
613-235-1566

Adoption Council of Ontario
134 Clifton Road
Toronto, Ontario M4T 2G6
416-482-0021

Adoptive Parents Association of Alberta
parent support group;
  member of Adoptive
  Families of America
Box 6496
Bonnyville, Alberta T9N 2H1
403-826-5625

Appendix B

~~~~~~

ADOPTION-FRIENDLY MENTAL HEALTH RESOURCES

MENTAL HEALTH SERVICES

Clearinghouse on Disability Information
Office of Special Education and Rehabilitative Services (OSERS)
Room 3132, Switzer Building
330 C Street SW
Washington, DC 20202-2524
202-732-1723

National Center for Youth with Disabilities (NCYD)
University of Minnesota
Box 721, UMHC
Minneapolis, MN 55455
800-333-6293

National Council of Independent Living Programs (NCILP)
Troy Atrium
Broadway & Fourth Street
Troy, NY 12180
518-274-7944

National Mental Health Association
800-969-6642

President's Committee on Employment of Persons with Disabilities
1111 20th Street NW
Washington, DC 20036-3470
202-653-5044

RESIDENTIAL CARE RESOURCES

American Association of Children's Residential Centers
1021 Prince Street
Alexandria, VA 22314
703-838-7522

Boys Town
Boys Town Center
Boys Town, NE 68010
402-498-1301

Child Welfare League of America
440 First Street
Washington, DC 20001-2085
202-638-2952

Devereux Foundation
19 S. Waterloo Road
Devon, PA 19333
215-964-3287;
   800-345-1292, ex. 3045

National Alliance of Private Residential Resources (NAPRR)
4200 Evergreen Lane
Suite 315
Annandale, VA 22003
703-642-6614

National Alliance for the Mentally Ill
2101 Wilson Boulevard
   Suite 200
Washington, DC 20006
202-223-3447

National Association of Psychiatric Treatment Centers for Children
2000 L Street N.W., Suite 200
Washington, DC 20036
202-935-3828

Appendix C

▀▀

CHILDREN'S HEALTH ORGANIZATIONS

Attention Deficit Disorder
Attention Deficit Disorder
    Association (ADDA)
800-487-2282

AIDS
National AIDS Hotline
800-342-2437
National AIDS Information
    Clearinghouse
800-458-5231

Birth Defects
March of Dimes Birth Defects
    Foundation National
    Headquarters
Community Services
    Department
1275 Mamaroneck Avenue
White Plains, NY 10605
914-428-7100

Blindness
The American Council of the
    Blind
800-424-8666

The National Society to Prevent
    Blindness
800-221-3004

Cancer
American Cancer Society
800-227-2345
Cancer Information Service
800-422-6237

Cleft Palate
American Cleft Palate
    Foundation
800-242-5338

Diabetes
American Diabetes Association
800-232-3472

Juvenile Diabetes Foundation
800-223-1138

Disabilities
Information Clearinghouse for
    Infants with Disabilities
800-922-9234

National Organization on
    Disability
800-248-2253

Doctor Accreditation
Doctor Certification Line
800-776-2378

Down Syndrome
National Down Syndrome
    Congress
800-232-6372

Drug Exposure
National Association for
    Perinatal Addiction Research
    and Education
800-638-2229

Dyslexia
Orton Dyslexia Society
800-222-3123

Epilepsy
Epilepsy Foundation of
    America
800-332-1000

General Health
National Health Information
    Center
800-336-4797

Genetics
National Alliance of Genetic
    Support Groups
800-336-4363

Hearing
Hearing and Speech Helpline
800-638-8255

Heart
American Heart Association
800-242-8721

Mental Health
National Mental Health
    Association
800-969-6642

Multiple Sclerosis
The Multiple Sclerosis
    Association of America
800-833-4672

Neurological
National Institute of
    Neurological Disorders
800-352-9424

Rare Disorders
National Organization for Rare
    Disorders
800-999-6673

SIDS
National Center for the
    Prevention of Sudden Infant
    Death Syndrome
800-638-7437

Spina Bifida
Spina Bifida Association of
    America
800-621-3141

Speech
American Speech-Language-
    Hearing Helpline
800-638-8255

National Center for Stuttering
800-221-2438

Appendix D

PEDIATRIC AND EDUCATIONAL ADVOCACY GROUPS

Adoptive Families of America
3333 Highway 100 North
Minneapolis, MN 55422
800-372-3300; 612-535-4829;
Fax 612-535-7808

Alliance of Genetic Support Groups
emphasis on genetic disorders
1001 22nd Street NW
Suite 800
Washington, DC 20037
800-GENE; 202-331-0942

Association of Jewish Families and Children
800-634-3678

Child Defense Fund
25 E Street NW
Washington, DC 20001
202-628-8787

Child Welfare League of America
440 First Street NW
Suite 310
Washington, DC 20001
800-275-2952

Coalition for America's Children
1634 Eye Street NW
12th Floor
Washington, DC 20006
202-638-5770

Coleman Advocates for Children & Youth
2601 Mission Street
Suite 804
San Francisco, CA 94110
415-641-4362

Concerned United Birthparents
link to other birthparents
800-822-2777

Family Resource Coalition
parent support group network
200 South Michigan Avenue
Suite 1520
Chicago, IL 60604
312-341-0900

**National Association of
  Child Advocates**
1625 K Street NW
Suite 510
Washington, DC 20006
202-828-6950

**National Black Child
  Development Institute**
1023 15th Street NW
Suite 600
Washington, DC 20005
202-387-1281; 800-556-2234

**National Parent Network on
  Disabilities**
1600 Prince Street
Suite 115
Alexandria, VA 22314
703-684-6763

**North American Council on
  Adoptable Children**
970 Raymond Avenue
Suite 106
St. Paul, MN 55114-1149
612-644-3036;
    Fax 612-644-9848

Parent Action
Two North Charles Street, #960
Baltimore, MD 21201
410-727-3687

**Parent Training and
  Information Center (PTI)**
contact your state's Department
of Education; free information about disabilities, educational rights of disabled
students, support services for
families, and the state's financial resources for families of
children with disabilities

**Single Parent Resource
  Center**
1165 Broadway, Room 504
New York, NY 10001
212-947-0221

**Stepfamily Association of
  America**
215 Centennial Mall South
Suite 212
Lincoln, NE 68508
402-477-STEP; 800-735-0239

Stepfamily Foundation
333 West End Avenue
New York, NY 10023
212-877-3244
212-799-STEP for recorded
  information
212-744-6924 for the 24-hour
  hotline

Toughlove
teen troubles
800-333-1069

INDEX